Making Sense of the Creeds

Making Sense of the Creeds

Rupert E. Davies

EPWORTH PRESS

British Library Cataloguing in Publication Data

Davies, Rupert E.
  Making sense of the creeds.
  1. Creeds
  I. Title
  238   BT990

  ISBN 0–7162–0433–9

First published 1987
by Epworth Press,
Room 195, 1 Central Buildings,
Westminster, London SW1H 9NR
Typeset at The Spartan Press Ltd
Lymington, Hants
and printed in Great Britain by
Richard Clay Ltd
Bungay, Suffolk

Contents

Preface

The creeds set out what Christians are supposed and expected to believe. But many churchgoing people justly complain that no one, from the pulpit or anywhere else, has given them a clear explanation of the statements which are found in the creeds, or a sensible defence of those parts which are not easy to accept.

I have a strong suspicion, also, that many people would come to church if they could be sure of being treated there with the same respect for their intelligence as they receive in their daily occupation.

This book has been written with both these groups of people especially in mind. The immediate stimulus to writing it was given to me by a group of people from country and town which met in Compton Martin, Avon, to study 'the use of the creeds'. I am very grateful to them.

I owe a great deal to Christine Lillington, who has coped successfully with the formidable task of typing my illegible script; and to Margaret, my wife, who has scrutinized every paragraph with great care.

There are no footnotes in this book. There could have been a great number, since there is a profusion of books and theories about every subject here touched upon. But I wanted the reader to have, as far as possible, an unimpeded journey through the book. Such a journey could, I venture to hope, be a prelude to group discussion of each chapter.

Bishopsworth, Bristol   *Rupert E. Davies*
September 1986

1 *The Creeds: what are they and how shall we read them?*

The creeds occupy a position of almost unquestioned sanctity in the life of the Christian church. They are said or sung in the liturgy of almost every part of it; they are among the foundation-documents of almost every denomination; they are taught as an essential part of preparation for confirmation or its equivalent in a great number of churches; and if a non-Christian asks for a summary of the principal tenets of the Christian Faith, where can he be sent for information except to the creeds?

Yet some parts of them are unintelligible to modern Christians, and some of the intelligible parts border on the incredible. They are couched in the language of the distant past and have no apparent contact with modern issues or with daily life. Taken either separately or as a whole, they go nowhere near to covering the whole range of Christian belief.

So what useful purpose do the creeds serve in the present day? When people speak of the creeds they usually mean the Apostles' Creed and the Nicene Creed; sometimes they include also the Athanasian Creed, and, occasionally, the Chalcedonian Definition. To lump all these together under the name 'creeds' is in fact quite misleading. They are all, undoubtedly, statements of Christian faith, or, at least, summaries of what Christians believe. But they are different in origin and purpose.

The Apostles' Creed is the oldest of them all. It is what is called a Baptismal Creed. When non-Christians – whether they were Jews or people whom Christians were pleased to call 'pagans' – decided to become Christians in the first two or three hundred years of the Christian church, they were taking a very momentous and dangerous step, with the prospect of being cut off from their families and all their old friends and associations – and at certain periods of being harassed and done to death by the authorities of the Roman Empire. They did not take this step lightly, nor could the church receive them lightly. Before they were baptized, they had to know what they were now expected to believe: and the church had to know that they honestly believed what they professed – it was always possible that they were government moles. So every convert had to make a public confession of faith. At first, in New Testament times, all the convert had to say in public was 'Jesus is Lord' – which was a much more important statement than it sounds, for to call anyone 'Lord' was to assert for him an authority over the human race which only a divine being could claim; and to call Jesus 'Lord' was to affirm that all the other claimants to the title, including the Roman Emperor himself, were bogus.

But this large and simple affirmation soon had to be spelt out as questions were asked, and the formulae which the candidates for baptism had to utter became more and more complicated. One fairly elaborate formula was already used in late New Testament times, and appears in I Tim. 3.16: the convert confessed his faith in Jesus, 'who was manifested in the body, vindicated in the spirit, seen by angels; who was proclaimed among the nations, believed in throughout the world, glorified in high heaven.' This particular statement does not seem to have enjoyed a very wide use, and the various centres of Christian life and worship drew up their own – often after writing round to other churches to ask what they were doing in the matter. A century after the crucifixion, the church in Rome, the capital of the Empire, was already becoming the chief centre of Christianity, and its baptismal formula was more and more accepted (with slight modifications, no doubt) by other churches. Here is the Roman summary of the faith, dating back to about AD 150:

> I believe in God Almighty; and in Christ Jesus, his only son, our Lord; who was born of the Holy Spirit and the Virgin Mary; who was crucified under Pontius Pilate and was buried; and the third day rose from the dead; who ascended into heaven; and sits on the right hand of the Father; whence he comes to judge the living and the dead. And in the Holy Ghost, the holy church, the remission of sins, the resurrection of the flesh, and the life everlasting.

This was refined and amplified in succeeding years, until in the eighth century it took the form that we know as 'The Apostles' Creed' – except that it still speaks of 'the resurrection of the *flesh*', not 'the resurrection of the body'. It became more and more widely used in the churches of Western Europe which accepted the Roman obedience, and after the Reformation in the Protestant churches also. It has been used very little in the Orthodox churches of the East. 'Flesh' was changed to 'body' (which is truer to Paul in I Corinthians 15) in a version issued by Henry VIII in 1453, and the change has remained in English Prayer Books.

So it is clear that this creed was not written by the apostles, in spite of its name, and the pleasant legend that Peter said 'I believe in God', and James added 'the Father Almighty', and John 'Maker of heaven and earth', and so on through the apostolic team until the creed was complete, has to be dropped. But it can be said to contain the gist of the apostles' teaching in its most straightforward form.

The 'Nicene Creed' was produced to meet different circumstances. In the early centuries Christianity could not have survived, humanly speaking, unless it had been able to face intellectual criticism as well as physical persecution. The 'defenders of the faith', or the 'Apologists' as they were called (they were aggressive, rather than apologetic in our sense of the word), set out to confute and sometimes to ridicule the many religions and philosophies current at the time by emphasizing, in the Jewish tradition, the oneness of God, and by going on to say that Jesus had fulfilled the prophecies of the Old Testament in a marvellous way. From defence against attack from without, Christian teachers gradually moved into controversy with other teachers within the church who seemed to them to be distorting the principles of the faith. The longest and bitterest argument was with various groups of thinkers who were given the general name of 'Gnostics' – people who claimed to have a special knowledge of ultimate reality, and whose knowledge usually took the form of asserting that physical life (including that of Jesus) and material things were to be discounted as grossly inferior to the pure life of the spirit which they claimed to live. Against this view, the great expositor of biblical theology was Irenaeus, who died in about AD 200.

Perhaps not many people outside the church were interested in the internal arguments, though no doubt the 'apologies' had a fairly wide circulation. But as Christianity moved into the centres of higher learning such as Alexandria and Antioch it found itself pitted against the most eminent and penetrating thinkers of the time. The dialogue which resulted was crucial, and the church owed its eventual triumph over the intellectual champions of paganism in no small measure to the way in which people like Clement and Origen made out their case at the turn of the second and third centuries.

The debate was of necessity conducted in the language and thought-forms of the current philosophy, loosely called 'Greek'. The original source of this lay in the writings of Plato, though Plato himself would not have recognized, and might well have disowned, many of its ideas; for Platonism over the centuries had been diluted by many concepts which came from Eastern religions and schemes of thought. Plato's primary conviction was that the world of physical and material things, apprehended by the senses, is transient and in the last analysis unimportant, while the world of invisible entities, discerned by pure intellect, is real and eternal; and this remained unchallenged. But the relation between the visible and the invisible worlds was depicted in many different ways, some of them bizarre in the extreme. The 'Neo-Platonists' of the third century were nearest to the thought of Plato himself; but they despised all material things as Plato did not, and introduced a mystical element into the discussion which belonged to their own age, not Plato's. This meant, among other things, that words like 'essence' (or 'being'), 'substance' and 'nature', in technical, philosophical senses, alien to the concrete language of the Bible, entered Christian theology, and became common coinage in intellectual circles. The Christian disputants tried hard to support their case by relating the 'new' language to the Bible, and Origen, who was the ablest biblical scholar of his time, was the most successful in doing this. But the valiant attempt to reconcile Christian faith with contemporary philosophy must have left many ordinary believers, even in the sophisticated city of Alexandria, with the sense that the Bible had been left far behind.

When the emperor Constantine, by the Edict of Milan in 313, declared toleration for all religions, the intellectual atmosphere of the Empire quickly changed. Constantine, although he did not make Christianity the official religion of the Empire, showed a marked preference for Christians and Christian worship, and it became 'the thing' to be a Christian if imperial favour was desired. This suited Constantine's book admirably, for his main aim in legalizing and favouring Christianity was the unity of his far-flung empire; his own Christian convictions were, to say the least, dubious, and did not greatly influence his personal life and political activities. The effect of the Edict was thus that Christian bishops began to be imperial potentates, and Christian beliefs became the orthodoxy of the ruling classes. Many people date the beginning of Christianity's decline from the policy of Constantine.

Then, to Constantine's extreme displeasure, the peace of the Empire was suddenly disrupted by the very people on whom he was relying to restore it and maintain it, the Christians. A clever priest in Alexandria, Arius, came out with his own version of Christianity. He argued that since Christ was the Son of God the Father, he must have come into existence later than the Father – as is normally the case in parenthood. At a certain point in time God the Father created Christ the Son, and later on the Son created the Holy Spirit. So there was a hierarchy of Father, Son and Holy Spirit; and Christ was not fully God – indeed, he was demi-God and demi-man. Arius quoted scriptural texts, and speciously claimed the support of Origen, for his contentions.

The person most infuriated by this compromise between Christianity and polytheism (for this is what it really was) was Athanasius, later to become Bishop of Alexandria, who had recently written a masterly treatise to show that Christ, the eternal, wholly divine Word had become man in order that we might become divine. Two parties were soon formed in Alexandria, with the alarming result that there was fighting in the streets, with each side shouting and singing slogans against the other. Constantine, afraid that this sort of thing would spread throughout the Empire, told the parties to stop wrangling, and when they failed to do this, he summoned all the bishops of the Eastern part of his Empire and some from the West to meet at Nicaea in Asia Minor in 325 and to settle the matter. He himself took the chair for many of the proceedings, and shared in the argument. The bishops (plus two priests from Rome) were anxious to please the Emperor, and agreed to accept the baptismal creed put forward by one of their number, Eusebius of Caesarea, as the statement of their common faith. But many thought it needed one addition to rule out the views of Arius: the phrase 'of one essence with the Father'. This was hotly disputed, until Constantine said that they must sign the revised document, or else. They then agreed.

This is what came out of the Council of Nicaea:

We believe in one God the Father all-sovereign, maker of all things visible and invisible; and in one Lord Jesus Christ, the Son of God, begotten of the Father, only begotten, that is, of the essence of the Father, God of God, Light of Light, true God of true God, begotten not made, of one essence with the Father, through whom all things were made, things in heaven and things on the earth; who for us men and for our salvation came down and was made flesh, and became man, suffered, and rose on the third day, ascended into heaven, is coming to judge living and dead. And in the Holy Spirit.

Notice that this is not our Nicene Creed, and that while there is a certain repetitiveness about Christ, it has virtually nothing to say about the Holy Spirit, or the church.

Constantine thought that he had resolved the issue for good and all. But he had not. Submerged discontents with the enforced formulation came quickly to the surface, parties were formed by bishops in many parts of the Empire to defend particular theories, many of them tending in an Arian direction, and local councils were held which repudiated the decisions of Nicaea. Constantine and his successors made vain efforts to keep the theological peace (after all, they needed time and energy to deal with invading barbarians on the Empire's frontiers) by backing what seemed the most powerful party at the time, and the various bishops schemed to gain the Emperor's ear. Confusion was worse confounded when the Empire was administratively divided into two, each under an emperor, and one emperor supported the Nicene party and the other the Arian party. Throughout it all Athanasius maintained the original statement of Nicaea, and was exiled four times for his pains by emperors who thought him a disturber of the peace (what peace?).

After fifty years passions cooled. Athanasius was dead, and even he had agreed to a mild compromise at the end of his life. The Emperor Theodosius, once again a sole emperor, called the bishops to Constantinople in 381, and under his direction they produced what we call the Nicene Creed, but which should properly be called the Nicaeno-Constantinopolitan Creed, probably based on the Baptismal Creed of the Church in Jerusalem. (This is the most likely account of rather obscure events.) The Arian issue was really settled this time: the relation of the Son to the Father, and of the Holy Spirit to both, within the oneness of the Trinity, was definitely stated. The Creed, which has survived in strength until today, came out of an amalgamation of philosophy, the Bible, and imperial and ecclesiastical politics – a remarkable combination and a remarkable result.

But argument about Christ was not yet over. It shifted from disputes about the Son and the Father and the Holy Spirit to disputes about the person of the Son, worshipped as both God and Man. How can he be both? Some teachers, like Nestorius, of Constantinople, emphasized his humanity; others, like Cyril, of Alexandria, emphasized his deity. This new dispute involved the same kind of ecclesiastical politics as had the Arian issue, for the powerful sees of Alexandria and Constantinople competed for authority in the Christian world and each desired imperial support. Once again the Emperor, this time Marcian, had to come into the arena, and at a great Council held at Chalcedon in Asia Minor in 451, following years of politicking, he presided over the promulgation of the 'Chalcedonian Definition'. This declared that Christ is to be 'recognized in two natures, without confusion, without change, without division, without separation; the distinction of natures being in no way annulled by the union, but rather the characteristics of each nature being preserved and coming together to form one person'.

The Definition largely followed the teaching of the influential Pope Leo I, but was not accepted by some of the churches in the East, such as those in Egypt and India, which remain separate from the rest of Christendom until this day. Perhaps because of this, and perhaps also because it states the problem without solving it, the Chalcedonian Definition has never had the acclaim accorded to the Nicene Creed, though it often counts as one of the creeds of the church.

The bishops of the church meeting in Constantinople and Chalcedon were concerned to deal with and refute what they believed to be untrue to Scripture and therefore false. The creeds which they produced deal with particular problems and set the boundaries within which Christian thought should operate in these matters. Thus we have gone far beyond the purpose of baptismal creeds.

The Athanasian Creed (sometimes called, from the opening Latin words, 'The Quicunque Vult') should not really rank among the creeds. It is neither a Baptismal Creed, nor a formulary produced by a Council. Nor indeed was it written by Athanasius, though it could be said in a general way to express his point of view. It could have been put together either in the fourth, or more probably in the fifth century, and was intended by its author (whoever he was) to confute certain heresies. It came into wide use in the worship of churches in the West, but never in the East, and in recent years it has gradually faded out of the picture (though it survives in the *Alternative Service Book* for certain specified occasions), largely because of the curses which it pronounces upon dissidents, as well as of its own uncongenial dogmatism.

What are we to make, in our time, of these ancient documents with their chequered origins, remembering that two of them at least, the Apostles' Creed and the Nicene Creed, have lasted through the centuries as definitive statements of Christian belief?

There seem to be four main possibilities:

(*a*) We can continue to affirm them, or at least the Apostles' and Nicene Creeds, literally and as they stand. This is the way in which Christians have used them through the centuries, and some Christians see no reason for changing the situation. But if we do this we are requiring belief in certain propositions which many Christians now find hard to believe: (*i*) Jesus Christ came down from heaven (as if it were 'up there'). (*ii*) He descended into the place of the departed (as if it were 'down there'). (*iii*) He

ascended back into heaven. (*iv*) He will come again from
there. (*v*) The Being (or Essence) of God the Father and God
the Son is one and the same (a sentence hard, surely, for
people today to understand, let alone believe).

But a more serious objection is that the awesome mystery
of God, and the infinite profundity of relations within the
Trinity, cannot really be encapsulated in a few brief
propositions – or in any proposition at all, however
carefully thought out.

(*b*) We can take the creeds to be generally authoritative,
but reserve the right to contract out of statements within
them which we find incredible. This could mean altering
the creeds for worship or encouraging people in public
worship to refrain from saying what they do not believe
(this latter course could have an odd result if there were a
gap of silence, or just a dull murmur, when certain clauses
were reached).

This would preserve the integrity of many Christians
who are at present made uncomfortable by being asked to
recite what they do not really believe. But it subjects the
creeds of the church to each person's private judgment; and
to omit particular phrases may well remove what is vital to
the unity of the whole (to remove the Second Coming, for
instance, would damage the total witness to the work of
Jesus).

(*c*) We can remove the creeds altogether from public
worship and the formularies of the church, and consider
them purely as historical documents, of interest only to
those who wish to form a complete picture of the life of the
early church. No doubt this would clear the decks of
Christian doctrine by discarding much apparently surplus
luggage, and relieve many Christian consciences. But,
quite apart from the fact that it would release a traditionalist
backlash of unprecedented ferocity, it would leave the

church at large without any agreed statement of belief on which it could begin to unite.

(*d*) On the assumption that the creeds, in their own way, assert universal Christian belief, we can dig beneath the words and thought-systems of the ancient Graeco-Roman world to discover what the creeds are basically saying, and then try to reassert the truths thus discovered in language which is intelligible and credible to modern minds.

There are, of course, dangers in this proposal also. In the process of carrying it out we might well miss the essential meaning while removing the words in which it is expressed, or we might entirely or partially fail to express that meaning in the 'new' language that we use. And in any case we should be justified in carrying out this method only if we acknowledged at the outset that the same criticism will of necessity be applied in due course to any language we use as we have ourselves applied to the language of the fourth century; and this, no doubt, after a much shorter lapse of time.

Nevertheless this is the method which we shall pursue in this book as likely to be the most productive and useful in the present time and, we hope, to help others to do better what has to be done.

Before we embark on it, two things must be made very clear. It is the unconscious practice of many Christians, especially those who say the Nicene Creed frequently, to understand the New Testament in the light of the creeds, as though the creeds had an extra special authority in the interpretation of scripture. This cannot be the right way to treat either scripture or the creeds. The Councils of the church, including those of Nicaea and Constantinople, certainly believed that they knew, and were expressing, the truths of scripture. But in view of the prolonged study of the Bible and its, in many cases, assured results, we must take leave to doubt whether the creeds always got the meaning of scripture exactly right. We shall therefore in this book seek to understand and to test the creeds in the light of scripture, and ask its readers to abandon the opposite procedure.

Then also we have to be clear that in the process we shall have to treat many of the statements in the creeds as *mythological*, and that word may set many people's hair on end. But 'mythological' does not mean 'untrue'. Quite the contrary. It is a word which points to a very important fact. We cannot state in logical terms, exactly and accurately, the fundamental truths about God and his relation to the world. Our minds are too puny, and our language hopelessly inadequate. So we are bound to use the best language that is available, and this is usually the language of poetry and parables and images – that is, in the proper sense of the term, *mythological language*, language which expresses great truths in imaginative forms. Apart from some obviously historical statements, the language of the creeds can best be understood as, *in this sense*, mythological, and it is in this way that we shall interpret it.

If it be said that the authors of the creeds intended to write not mythologically but exactly, and had no idea that their words would be mythologically interpreted, this may well be true. But the exact language of one age is often seen to be mythological by a later one as we discover both the limits and the strength of the words that have been used. This is as often the case with the sciences, such as physics and psychology, as with theology. It cannot surely be held that the *id*, the *ego* and the *superego* of Freudian orthodoxy are actual entities within the human psyche. And in theology the supreme example is the Bible itself, where for instance, the stories of creation, no doubt intended as literal descriptions, can now be much more profitably, and truthfully, acclaimed as myths.

We shall focus our attention on the Nicene Creed (usually just calling it 'the Creed'), and use the others for illustration and amplification.

The texts of the Apostles' Creed, the Nicene Creed and the Chalcedonian Definition are set out in the Appendix at the end of the book.

2 We believe in one God, the Father, the Almighty, maker of heaven and earth, and of all things visible and invisible

'*We*'. The first word is important. For no very good reason many prayer books, including the Book of Common Prayer, changed the 'we' of the original to 'I'. This had the effect of turning the Creed into an individual profession of belief made while each other member of the congregation is doing the same. It misses the corporateness of the original, in which first the Council of Constantinople, and, since then, innumerable congregations in all parts of the Church Catholic down the ages, have professed their common faith. The *Methodist Service Book* and the *Alternative Service Book*, among many others, have now restored the original 'we'. And to say 'we' may perhaps help any members of a congregation who are doubtful about their belief in one or other of the clauses or words to join with their fellow-worshippers in a common affirmation of Christian faith, without committing themselves to every item of it. But others will think that this is a dishonest evasion of the issue!

'*We believe in one God*'. In original intention, no doubt, the Council was simply saying 'we *believe that* there is one God, the Almighty, maker of heaven and earth', and so on. It was a statement of intellectual assent. And this is, of course, how it can still be used, and usually is.

But the New Testament gives a deeper sense of 'believing in' (as distinct from just 'believing that'); those who *believe in* God through Christ have committed themselves to him as their Lord, and entrusted themselves to him for this life and the next. We can *believe that* God exists without doing anything whatever to put that belief into practice – and many people do exactly that. We can believe that the whole of Christian doctrine is true, and, similarly, do nothing whatever about it. But, surely, it is a much more genuine act of worship if we confess our *belief in* God at a deeper level than intellectual assent. It could even be that believing in God at this deeper level helps many people to resolve the problems which trouble them at the intellectual level – and this is good, so long as it does not land them in trying to avoid difficult questions. 'We believe, in order that we may understand' said St Anselm.

'In one God'. The Council made this uncompromising assertion that there is only one God in the face of two sets of opponents. Jewish teachers maintained that Christians had turned away from the monotheism of the Old Testament to polytheism by holding the doctrine of the Trinity, which, it seemed, included three gods. The Creed comes out directly with an assertion of monotheism against its Jewish critics, and amplifies this later by what it says about Jesus Christ and the Holy Spirit.

The controversy with the Jews is one that has required full understanding and careful argument from both sides. It is sad that the Christian church in the succeeding centuries avoided the argument by the absurd statement that 'all Jews are guilty of the murder of Jesus', which has embittered Jewish-Christian relations ever since; and the hurt is only now being healed, though sensible Christians have long ago given up the cruel and unjust accusation.

The other opponents held in mind by the Council were the adherents of the myriad non-Christian faiths which stated that there were two gods, or more, and sometimes many more. The general temper of the times was to accept the existence of a multiplicity of deities, male and female, and to allow each individual sect to worship as it wished, so long as it did not disturb the peace of the Empire by denying the deity of the Emperor himself. Sometimes it was held, in educated circles, that all the various gods and goddesses were manifestations of the one supreme Deity, so that one could have the best of all worlds by a philosophical belief in the unity of God, while practising the particular religion of one's fancy.

Most pervasive of all were the religions which held that there were two gods, one creating good and the other creating evil, engaged in perpetual conflict with each other. This notion went back to the teaching of Zarathustra, the Iranian teacher who spoke of Ormuzd (good) and Ahriman (bad); and Manichaeism, which held that all matter was evil, and only spirit was good, was another religion of the same sort.

Our situation is different. We are rarely confronted by people who claim to believe in many gods, but often by those who say that there is no god at all. It should be said, however, that atheism easily leads to a modern kind of polytheism. When belief in one God ceases, the field is open for any number of deities to take over the control of human minds and imaginations – not only in the form of strange cults but also in various types of materialism and sensuality. And the 'dark gods', which sometimes seem to all of us to lurk below the level of consciousness, rise to the surface, attempt to take control, and effectively disperse our energies in many different directions at the same time as we try to come to terms with ourselves. So polytheism is by no means dead and gone.

But real atheism is also to be found in many parts of the West. It has often been shown that it was not until the Christian belief in one God had taken firm hold of the human mind in Europe (perhaps not until the time of the Renaissance and Reformation) that science as we know it was possible, for it presupposes the orderliness of the universe – a cosmos not a chaos. It may be that if atheism prevails, and everything in the universe is ascribed to the workings of chance, science cannot survive for long. So the Creed's assertion of monotheism is highly relevant in more than one way to our times. What the Creed asserts, then, against both polytheism and atheism, is that the entire universe is under one rule and one only; and that therefore one mind with one purpose informs and gives meaning to everything that is.

In fact the great majority of the human race believe in God; under any number of names – Allah, Karma, Ultimate Reality, the Absolute, the eternal values, the All, and many more. So the assertion that there is one God means also that when people worship God (or gods) under any name whatever, they are worshipping the one God. It is common to talk of worshipping 'another God'; we sometimes dispose of other faiths in this way, which suggests that the 'other gods' do not really exist at all. But it is a false and confusing way of speaking. Muslims, Sikhs, Rastafarians, Shahmanists, polytheists, and all other worshippers, worship the only God that there is to worship, though they do so with many different concepts and ceremonies and ethical systems.

The Creed in its next assertion sets out to show, so far as it can be shown, what we can truly say about this one God, and it nails its colours to a particular mast.

'*The Father, the Almighty*'. Any Christian description of God must accept the word 'Father' as basic, since it is the word that Jesus most commonly used to describe God's relationship with himself and with all of us. 'Father' to him was not a sentimental word; it did not denote any softness or tendency to indulgence. A Jewish father was the source of both affection and authority towards all other members of the family. His word was final, and his love was constant. There was no other word in Jewish language that could be applied to God with anything like equal force or meaning.

But this does not mean that the word 'Father' is adequate to describe the character of God, for there is no word of which that can be said. To call God 'Father' is to ascribe to him all the best qualities ever found in human fatherhood and to assert their presence in him to an infinite degree. Above all, it serves to indicate that God is at least personal – not a person (for that would subject him to the limitations of an individual person), but personal; which means, above all, that he enters into personal relations with his human creatures and calls forth a personal response from them to him. But to call him 'Father' also points to his constant care for each of his creatures, so that not even a sparrow falls to the ground without his knowledge. The wicked are as valuable to him as the virtuous, and his wish to provide the very best for each of them never ceases.

But in the history of the Christian church the word Father, as applied to God, has acquired some overtones which are not faithful to the teaching of Jesus. In Christian art and Christian literature, and usually in Christian theology, God the Father has been depicted as male. Perhaps there seemed to be no other way to do it, but the effect of this on the Christian mind is that we have all come to think of him exclusively in male terms. Also, the society

in which most Christians have lived has been uninterrupt-
edly patriarchal, and we have unconsciously transferred to
God the attributes of a 'father' as the surrounding society
has conceived him. No one will admit that he or she thinks
of God as male; nearly everyone would repudiate such a
notion. But the language which we use, especially the
language of worship, prayer and hymns, and the art which
we appreciate, influence us in our inward attitudes and
concepts far more than we care to admit; and, whether we
wish it or not, God is to us a *male* person; a person of infinite
power and love – but exclusively male. There have been
protests against this in writers like Anselm and Julian of
Norwich, but they have not been very effective.

Therefore we need to remember that the Old Testament,
and Jesus himself, compare God also with a mother; and to
correct the image of God in our own minds, even as we use
the word 'Father', by ascribing to him (or him/her, as some
would prefer to say) the highest qualities of motherhood to
an infinite degree as well as those of fatherhood. John
Calvin modified his somewhat harsh delineation of God by
saying that all images of God are inadequate, and that it is
perfectly legitimate to use the image of motherhood as well
as that of fatherhood when speaking of him, since Jesus
himself did so.

'*The Almighty*'. It might have been better if the translators
had translated the word that is in the original Greek, rather
than the word in the Latin translation, and asked us to say
'All-Sovereign' rather than 'Almighty'. The Greek word
'Pantocrator' affirms that God is in supreme control of the
universe. The Latin word 'Omnipotens' – omnipotent,
almighty – has the same meaning, 'possessing all power', in
its original use. But it has come to mean something different.

When we say that God is almighty we usually mean that
he can do everything, *and that he in fact does everything that he*

can. From this the conclusion has been easily drawn that, since God does everything he can and he is in charge of the world, everything that happens is God's doing. So when a child died in Victorian days of a disease that we can now cure, or indeed of one that we cannot yet cure, the parents were expected to believe that his death was God's will, and duly inscribed that belief on the child's tombstone.

It is a blasphemous belief, but if we assume that God does everything he can, we may be driven to it by sheer logic; just as Calvin was driven by sheer logic, of which he was a master, to the belief, horrible though it was, that all human beings are destined by God from the beginning of time either to damnation or to salvation.

If we look again at the New Testament we shall find that this is not at all what we are required to believe, though we shall admit that a few passages tend in that direction. The whole work and teaching of Jesus imply that God's grace is offered to all without exception, and that no one can possibly be damned in advance. And if this is so, we are bound to say – and, surely, happy to say – that God, though he has all power (including, no doubt, the power to damn and to save), does not in fact do all that he has the power to do – that, like any good father (or mother), he does not coerce his human creatures into obedience, but encourages them to exercise their freedom; and if they use that freedom in the wrong way, he is willing to forgive and forbear to the limit.

In other words, omnipotence does not mean 'omni-performance'; God's use of his infinite power is governed by his infinite love. We are to interpret his 'almightiness' in the terms of his fatherhood, and not the other way round.

When we say all this to ourselves and to others, we are at once reminded of the Mexican earthquake, the Chernobyl disaster, the spread of AIDS, and the innumerable other evils, some caused by human error or sin, some without any apparent human causation, which afflict the human race. If God is 'the Father, the Almighty', why does he allow these things to happen? We cannot evade the 'problem of evil'. There is no conclusive answer to it, and attempts to provide an answer are bound to seem facile and superficial.

But some things can be said. We do not extricate ourselves from the difficulty by saying that God is evil, or that he does not exist. We simply land ourselves with other problems. If God is evil, why is there so much good in the world? If God does not exist, how can we explain *either* good *or* evil?

These two problems are even more difficult to solve than the problem of evil for the Christian. It is, surely, the very nature of evil to suppress and abolish good; indeed, if God were evil he would not allow it to exist at all. Yet the amount of good in the world is immense, though we take most of it for granted. There is not only goodness in people, but also goodness in human societies, on a very large scale; and there seem to be no people and no societies from which good is entirely absent. Nor do the constant efforts of evil people to eradicate good ever quite succeed. An evil God would surely by now have eliminated this challenge to his rule if he had ever allowed it to be made in the first place.

If there is no God, and the universe is a concatenation of things brought together by chance, the words 'evil' and 'good' have no meaning at all. There are things which we like, and things which we dislike, and that is all that can be said. But the concepts of 'good' and 'evil' are ineradicable elements of the human mind; we cannot hold that they are meaningless without calling into question every thought we ever think, and reducing the human race to a set of automata.

But if God is good, we must expect him to allow evil; for if he did not, there would be no such thing as freedom. No one really doubts that a good God is of his very nature to be expected to grant freedom. But if we are to have freedom, the universe in which we have to exercise it must be a stable and reliable one, proceeding in accordance with principles and laws which are capable of being discovered and which operate without interruption. Freedom would be useless and meaningless unless the same cause always had the same effect, unless the sun were bound to rise and the night to fall.

Freedom, then, requires the possibility of evil and the reliability of scientific laws. It may often seem to us that the price to be paid for freedom in terms of actual evil is a very heavy one – and here remains the difficulty. But some light is thrown on even this difficulty if we remember that God is all-sovereign; that the universe, including 'the time of this mortal life' and beyond, is in his hands, and that he has full scope in eternity for the final execution of his loving purposes for the human race.

'Maker of heaven and earth, and of all things visible and invisible.' The phrase 'maker of heaven and earth' comes in both the Apostles' Creed and the Nicene Creed. For the authors, the universe was a three-storeyed affair: heaven above, where God and the angels and the saints live; the earth, where we are; and Hades (or Sheol) the place under the earth, where the souls of the once-living stay until the final resurrection. 'The earth' in the Creed includes the place beneath it. God is the maker of all three places.

Then comes a phrase from contemporary philosophy, 'all things visible and invisible'. Beyond the world of visible objects, animals and people – the whole physical universe, in fact – is the *in*visible world of 'being' or 'essence'. This invisible world gives such meaning as there is to the visible world. God, says the Creed, is the creator of both the visible and the invisible worlds, which together comprise everything that is.

We no longer think in any of these terms, but we certainly do not wish to deny the creatorhood of God. We are best able to gain the truth behind the language if we affirm that God is the creator of the entire universe, however vast that universe is (and we do not yet know how vast that is), and leave the matter there.

But the words 'creator' and 'create' are no longer clear to us. Some Christians think that they are tied by their faith to the narrative of the earliest events that is to be found in Genesis (actually there are two narratives in Genesis, which do not agree with each other); and that they are therefore expected to believe that God created the universe and everything in it within the space of six days. Others are prepared to jettison the chronology and the exact order of events given by Genesis, but suppose that it is a requirement of faith to believe that the universe was created once and for all at the beginning of time.

But both these views are misunderstandings of the Genesis myth. This is not concerned with precise events or dates, or with chronological order; or with the question of how long it took God to create the world. It states (with a wealth of detail which belongs to the story told, and not to the truth conveyed) that the universe depends for its existence, and the existence of everything in it, on God; without him it would not exist at all: and if at any time he ceased to will its existence, it would thereupon cease to exist forthwith. God's creation is 'out of nothing'; it is not out of pre-existent matter. Before the creation there was *nothing*, except God.

Scientists will, and must continue to work out and test theories of the way in which the world and the other occupants of space came into existence, and the question is for many people, of course, one of absorbing interest. But the inquiry does not affect the statement in the Creed. In recent years the 'big bang' theory has gained some support among Christians because it seems to tally with Genesis; but this apparent general similarity neither supports the Christian view of creation, nor does it weaken it. The 'steady state' theory is equally a matter of scientific interest which does not touch the theological issues. Genesis, and the Bible in general, does not purport to show *how* God created the world. Its concern is to affirm that it is *God* who created it.

But there are scriptural statements which we can add to the myth of Genesis. These are to the effect that God is still at this moment active in creation (see Isaiah Ch. 40) and never ceases from his creative activity. If so, every child born, every poem written, every 'new thing' that appears in our world, is God's creation. In any case it is clear, from the basic doctrine of creation, that God sustains the universe in being; we can also affirm that God is still creating the universe. So we are certainly not bound down to the view that God created the universe billions of aeons ago and then stopped creating.

The universe, then, is the result of God's creative activity. Christians have been inclined, while freely admitting this truth, to suppose that the creation of the human race was so important that all other parts of creation pale into insignificance, or that the rest of creation in the last resort exists solely for our convenience. Hence the squandering of the earth's resources for human purposes; hence the destruction of life in animals and plants which do not happen to suit what we believe to be our welfare. Even those who are in favour of conservation sometimes suggest that this should be carried out chiefly for human benefit.

But the entire universe is God's creation, and every part of it, not just humankind, is important to him. We are latecomers on the scene of the universe; we have no right to suppose that it is maintained solely, or even mainly, for our benefit. Certainly we have gifts which other members of the creation do not have, or do not have in so great a measure. This gives us advantages which we are very quick to exploit, often to destructive effect; but it also gives us responsibilities, from the Christian point of view, to the rest of the universe, which so far we have been very slow to carry out.

Thus the Creed, under its archaic language, states a cosmology and an ecology which involve no conflict with our scientific knowledge of the world. The ecology is one which can even ease, in a small measure, the nagging problem of evil. We tend to judge all the events that happen in the universe from a human point of view: if they are helpful to us, they are good; if they harm us, they are bad. But on the Creed's account of God's economy, this is a very narrow view. Indeed, it may be necessary for us, with our extra advantages and extra responsibilities, to suffer for the sake of the creation as a whole, as Jesus suffered for us. For we have the assurance, as the rest of creation (as far as we know) has not, that God the Father is all-sovereign and that all things are under his ultimate loving control.

3 We believe in one Lord, Jesus Christ, the only Son of God. . . .

Up to this point the Nicene Creed has followed the outline of the Apostles' Creed. But now, having reached the mention of Jesus Christ, it proceeds to elaborate its account of him with a profusion of phrases intended to exalt him to the highest possible dignity and authority, and to show his intimate relationship with the Father.

The reason for this is, of course, the controversy in which the authors of the creed had engaged: Arius and his friends had degraded Jesus to the position of a created being, a little higher, perhaps, than the angels, but distinctly lower than God. So the bishops both at Nicaea and at Constantinople were determined to assert, beyond any possibility of misunderstanding, the equality of God the Son with God the Father.

No doubt, if the task of doing this had been laid upon most modern thinkers, they would not have begun with high-sounding titles betokening full deity, but with an account of a human life which led to death on a cross and to resurrection from the dead. For us, in our time, the claim of Christ to deity springs chiefly from what he was, and said, and did, and is; it is on the basis of his life and death and rising again for us, and for the whole human race, that each of us says 'My Lord and my God'. Most probably, as this quotation from the words of Thomas in John's Gospel indicates, the same was true of the apostles.

But the Christian philosophers whose writings and words had led to the formulation of the Nicene Creed began at the other end. Of course, they would not have been able to say what they say about Jesus, the Son of God, unless they had been fully aware of his life and his saving work; but their order of thinking was dictated not by this, but the paramount need, as they saw it, to state clearly the relation of Jesus Christ to the Godhead, and to put Arius once and for all out of court.

This is one of the things that make the Nicene Creed difficult for us. In our forms of worship – and in this book – we have to follow the order prescribed by the Creed, but we do it somewhat against our will. The best way for us to surmount this difficulty and to restore the balance is to say (to ourselves), as we recite or reflect upon the sonorous phrases at the beginning of the paragraph: 'This Jesus of whom we are speaking in these strange terms is Jesus of Nazareth, who lived his life and gave himself to death for our sakes, and was raised by God from the dead, and has drawn from us our love and worship.'

'*One Lord, Jesus Christ*'. An echo of the primitive Baptismal Creed, 'Jesus is Lord'. But, still more, it gives to Jesus the highest title (in Greek *kyrios*) which the ancient world could offer to anyone, equivalent to the Hebrew word Jahweh, which we often translate 'Lord'. Paul in Philippians (2.11) asserts that the title belongs to Jesus because of his humility and his obedience to death on a cross, and elsewhere he says that though there are many 'gods' and many 'lords', 'yet for us there is one God, the Father, from whom all being comes, towards whom we move; and there is one Lord, Jesus Christ, through whom all things came to be, and we through him' (I Cor. 8.6).

In the years between Paul and the Council of Nicaea, Jesus Christ had been competing with the many 'lords' which were asserted to exist, and especially with the Emperor's lordship – and he, of course, when he decided to assert himself, was the most puissant lord of all, for he had the power of life and death.

But when the bishops met at Nicaea the victory of Christ was, it seemed, assured, and could be confidently asserted. The old gods and goddesses of the Mediterranean world had faded away, as the Emperor Julian found to his cost when he tried to revive them in his reaction against Christianity in the middle of the fourth century.

One rival indeed was still in the field, the Lord Mithra, the 'Invincible Sun', an Iranian deity, young and strong in people's minds, whom some of the emperors had tried to enthrone as the Supreme Deity of the Roman Empire. Mithra's worshippers celebrated their Lord's birthday on December 25, and communed with him in a sacred meal which included drinking the blood of a slaughtered bull. The armies of the Empire were attracted to his worship in large numbers, not least in Britain, where they could be observed 'worshipping the rising sun' (perhaps with the more enthusiasm because of its rare appearance in that foggy land). There were shrines to him all over the Empire, and in Britain in such widely separated places as London, Hadrian's Wall and Brean Down near Weston-super-Mare.

But by the time of Constantine, Mithraism also was rapidly declining, chiefly, perhaps, because it was strictly for men only. Religions which give a low place, but a place, to half the human race, like Christianity during most of its history until now, are known to survive, although they may not find it so easy in the future;

religions which exclude women completely, like Mithraism, have always been less likely to do so.

So when the Councils declared the sole lordship of Jesus
Christ, they did not expect to encounter a great deal of
opposition. The common Christian opinion, that the gods
and goddesses were either demons in disguise or non-
existent, held general sway, except in isolated pockets of
the countryside.

With us it is different. In our pluralist society, the Lord
Buddha and the Lord Siva have very many adherents,
while Muslims and Sikhs form many powerful and
growing communities; and we find that all these religions
encourage and exhibit virtues of character, and express
perceptions of truth, which we know that we can no
longer despise. Can we still acclaim Jesus as the 'One
Lord'?

All Christians are more or less agreed that the time has
come for 'dialogue' between Christians and those of 'other
faiths'. But the word 'dialogue' is differently interpreted in
different Christian circles. For some it is a prelude to the
resumption of old-style evangelism (or 'proselytism', as its
critics call it), designed to persuade non-Christians to
abjure their own faith and turn whole-heartedly to Christianity. They can quote scripture to this effect: 'There is no
salvation in anyone else at all, for there is no other name
under heaven granted to men, by which we may receive
salvation' (Peter's words as given in Acts 4.12).

But other Christians are no longer satisfied with this
approach. It seems to deny all virtue and truth to non-
Christians against all the evidence, and to contradict the
other biblical statement which speaks of 'the light which
enlightens every human being' (John 1.9). The purpose of
'dialogue' for them is not to cause others to abandon their
own faith, but rather mutual understanding between

Christians and non-Christians, both in the areas where they agree and in those where they do not.

The old 'monopolistic' view of the uniqueness of Christ is still strongly held, but there are many other schools of Christian thought at present on the subject. Some, in strong reaction against exclusiveness and narrowness, put all religions, or at least all the 'great' religions, on a level: Christ for the Western world, Jahweh for the Jews, Mohamet for the Arabs and many of the Asians, and so on. Each great teacher in the search for truth has found certain aspects of it, and each aspect is equally valid. Different people, and peoples, will opt for this teacher or that as 'the greatest', but all must treat each other with respect, and refrain from claiming absoluteness for any one faith. This is in the spirit of the Roman emperor Alexander who set up statues of Abraham, Orpheus, Apollonius (a second-century miracle-worker) and Christ in his private chapel, and of the modern independent school in the Midlands where Christian worship is (or was until recently) conducted in a hall which contains a similar but more contemporary set of statues. But it is clearly difficult to square this approach with either the Bible or the creeds; it surely denies the title of 'one Lord' to Christ.

If we are still to speak of the sole Lordship of Christ, in harmony with the Creed, we may do it in either of two different ways – in either case acknowledging with gratitude to God that he has granted to people of non-Christian faiths (in which we should include not only those which come to us from the Middle and Far East, but those also which come from Africa) many revelations of truth which can enrich our own understanding of God and of ourselves.

With this in mind, we can say that the same Christ whom we worship is present in every religion where God is truly worshipped and faith is sincerely held. To us he has been openly revealed, to others he is still concealed, but nevertheless at work among them. And it is through Christ, who is our Saviour from sin as well as the revealer of truth, that all those who believe in God receive forgiveness and new life. For *he* is the light which enlightens every human being; he is the light which shines in the dark, and the darkness has never mastered it (John 1.5); and it is in his name, even though that name be unknown to those who benefit from it, that all can be saved.

Or we can say that Jesus Christ *fulfils* all non-Christian faiths. Just as the Law and Prophets of the Old Testament were a 'preparation for the Gospel', so are the other faiths and the other prophets. In the case of the Old Testament, we have been aware of this from the beginning, since Jesus himself was a Jew, and inherited and developed the Jewish tradition of faith. That tradition of faith has handed on to the Christian church the special treasure of the oneness and the sovereignty of God which is still the pride of the Jewish church. Until recently, Christians have been barred, or have barred themselves, from appreciating the truths which are in other religions also, but now they can see that the Lord Buddha in his compassion, Mohamet in his insistence on submission to the divine will, and other prophets in their various ways, have brought to us a knowledge of God and of his relation to ourselves which otherwise we should never have appreciated quite so fully. All these religions, as they soon discover in dialogue with each other, have certain truths in common; but also at certain points contradict each other. They are all therefore incomplete – until they are fulfilled in Christ who accepts and develops the truths which they offer, removes the discrepancies where this is possible and shows the way to the elimination of the errors which have crept into all. Not that the fulfilment is yet accomplished, since Christ's teaching is not a rigid body of doctrine which stands for ever, but rather, both his teaching and his life still need to be explored over the centuries. And in this exploration people of all faiths are now able to share.

It certainly cannot be said that any account of the relation of Christianity, with its assertion of the sole lordship of Christ, to other faiths which do not yet accept it, is without difficulty and beyond question; we are only just beginning even to grasp the importance of the problem. But no Christian, we may hope, still accepts the statement of the Athanasian Creed: 'Whosoever will be saved; before all things it is necessary that he hold the Catholic Faith; which Faith except everyone do keep whole and undefiled: without doubt he shall perish everlastingly.'

'*The only Son of God, eternally begotten of the Father*'. At this point the Creed precipitates us into the doctrine of the Trinity. For many people this is a wholly unnecessary doctrine, and an unnecessarily complex doctrine at that. If only the church had confined itself to the simple gospel of Jesus, we should not have had to talk about the Trinity, and all the arguments and conflicts and puzzlements about it would not have arisen, they expostulate.

But this does not hold water. The 'simple gospel of Jesus' contains statements about the relationship of Jesus himself to his heavenly father which open up a whole world of profound thought. And once the early church was convinced, as it was as early as the writing of most of the books of the New Testament, that Jesus was in fact not only human but also divine – the Word of God, the Son of God – the question of his relationship with the Father became even more pressing and complex for those who loved God with their mind as well as their heart.

Here we have already the seeds of Trinitarian doctrine. It is quite true that the New Testament nowhere states the doctrine of the Trinity, although it contains much of the evidence for it. Yet when reflection on Jesus and the Father was further complicated by the conviction that the Spirit was guiding the church and empowering its members in the way in which only a divine being could (and there are examples of this conviction in the New Testament), the doctrine of the Trinity was well on the way to formulation and already becoming the subject of controversy.

But the doctrine has deeper roots than the demands of the Christian intellect. These roots lie in Christian experience – the experience of the community of the church and the experience of individual Christians, and it is not too much to say that in this regard the experience of the early Christians tallies with our own. They knew God as creator and sovereign; this was an inalienable part of their Jewish heritage. But they knew him also as a personal being whom they called Father (as the Jews themselves had begun to describe him) – a personal being in a personal relationship with themselves. They could speak of his care, and of his presence with them in their times of need. This experience was different from the consciousness of being at one with an all-pervasive reality which was common to most religions and was taken up into Christianity. It was *personal* and particular, and helped them to speak of God as Father in the way in which Jesus did, and as he had taught them to speak in the Lord's Prayer. This was an experience, as we now know, that was not peculiar to Christianity; but it was integral to Christianity.

But Jesus also was a personal being. That was obvious enough while he was alive on earth, but it is the testimony of the early church that it was still obvious after his death; whatever else we may say about the resurrection of Jesus, there is clear evidence that the apostles and their disciples, and their disciples' disciples, were aware of a personal relationship with a living Christ.

Experience of the Holy Spirit as personal came much later into focus, and there are Christians today who would prefer to speak of the Spirit of Jesus (as the Book of Acts sometimes does), or of Jesus as the Spirit (as the New Testament sometimes implies), than of the Spirit as a distinctive personal being. But the Spirit also, in the strong opinion of many, was experienced in personal encounter, and the view eventually prevailed that the Holy Spirit also is an eternal personal being.

All this amounted to a rather embarrassing discovery by the early writers on Christian theology. Here we have to reckon with three personal divine beings, they found; but they dared not, and would not ever, compromise the monotheism which is central both to the Old Testament and to the faith of the apostles.

So the church was forced into a doctrine of the Trinity by its own experience of God as well as by its theological reasoning. It arrived at such a doctrine reluctantly but inevitably. The Nicene Creed, stimulated, of course, by the opposition of Arius and the others who were willing to subside into a modified polytheism, represents a fully considered attempt to state as a truth of the Christian faith that God is three in one and one in three. The creed of Nicaea had set out an account of the relationship between the Father and the Son, and left the Holy Spirit 'hanging in the air'. The Nicene Creed grappled also with the relationship of the Holy Spirit with the Father and the Son.

Nevertheless, still in the interests of simplicity, many have argued that all we have to do is to say that there is one God, and that Father, Son and Holy Spirit are 'aspects' or, as the ancients would say, 'modes of being' of the one God. There was indeed a powerful body of Christian thinkers, known as Sabellians, in the third century, who took this line. But it will not really do. For we cannot affirm with any meaning or persuasiveness that we have communion with, or are aware of the presence of, an *aspect* (or mode); this is not the language or the nature of personal religion. The nub of the Nicene Creed's approach to the problem lies in the area of personal relationships. When we in our time speak of a 'person' or of 'personality', we have in mind the complex developing wholeness of the self as we hopefully find it within ourselves. This is a modern way of analyzing the word. The Fathers at Nicaea worked with a narrower, more static meaning of the word which we translate 'person'. But the meaning which they attached to the word is on the way to the meaning which is familiar to us; their meaning can be roughly given as 'the concrete reality which marks each of us out as an individual'.

Thus we find in the Creed the incipient idea of the Trinity as a community of persons; one community, three persons. To think of God as a community seems at first sight to make the Godhead *less than* personal – which is exactly what we do not wish to do. But what we are really saying is that the unity of God is far richer and deeper and more complex than any unity we can conceive: it is a unity which comprises and harmonizes three distinct persons, and remains nonetheless, or rather, far more, a real eternal unity, the perfect community.

Those who wrote the Creed did not have at their disposal nearly as many words as we have for a description of personality or of personal relationships. They first of all made use of terms which Jesus himself suggested, and Paul had taken up and developed: the terms of fatherhood and sonship. Jesus, then, could be called 'the only Son of God'. This phrase does not deny that in a different sense we are all called and enabled to be sons and daughters of God: he has accepted us into his family and loves us as a father does. It says, rather, that if we think of the closest possible relationship in human life as it was known to the ancients, we shall light on the relationship of an only son with his father (not of that between husband and wife – the ancients did not think like this about marriage); and that then we shall have some inkling of the relationship between the Son and the Father.

'*Eternally begotten of the Father*'. Those who wish to believe the Nicene Creed with absolute literalness are bound to be taken aback by this phrase! It can scarcely be the contention of the Creed that God the Father literally 'begat' Jesus! Jesus *is* the son of the Father, as we have just seen; but whereas (obviously) in human life the father's life precedes that of his son (the point which Arius had seized upon), in the divine life the relationship of Father and Son is eternal, without beginning and without end. Of course, this is all mythological – indeed the use of mythology is stretched to its limit to describe the intimacy of a divine relationship.

'*God of God, Light of Light, true God of true God*'. You may think that the Fathers of the Councils could not leave well alone; they hammer home the truth with blow after blow – a kind of theological overkill. But they still had the errors and machinations of the Arians in mind, and did not wish to leave them any way of escape. There is to be no doubt left anywhere at all, under any name, that Christ is divine, eternal, and eternally in union with God the Father.

'*Begotten, not made*'. A direct rebuttal of Arius, or anyone else who made Christ out to be part of the created universe.

'*Of one Being with the Father*'. And now we come to the *coup de grâce*! Yet perhaps it would have been as well if the Councils had left well alone at this point, for this phrase (which is one word in Greek and in its Latin translation) has caused more trouble and strife and perplexity than any other word in the Christian vocabulary. The first objection – which has to be upheld – made by its critics was that it is not to be found in scripture. But many others followed. And we have to ask: 'Was it – is it – worth all the trouble it has caused?'

We may as well set down the original word in all its mystery: *homoousios*. We must notice at once that we have now gone over from the language of scripture to that of philosophy. It was held by virtually all philosophers, and echoed in the language of all educated people, that to every category of thing or person there is an *ousia*, an 'essence' or 'form of being', in virtue of which a thing is what it is and nothing else, and he or she is who he or she is and no one else. There is therefore an 'ousia', an 'essence', of humanity, which is that in virtue of which we are human beings; and an 'ousia', or 'essence', of deity in virtue of which God is God. To use the phrase about Christ that he is 'of one being (or essence)' with the Father is to assert that the 'essence' of the Father and the 'essence' of the Son is *one and the same essence*; there is *one divine essence* in virtue of which they are what they are. It was the great concern of the Councils of Nicaea and Constantinople to exalt Christ as high as he can possibly be exalted in human language. And this is the way they chose. Whether all those present and voting in the Councils understood the subtlety of the statement is doubtful, but all must have been well aware that its intention was to ascribe full deity to Christ.

We no longer believe in 'essences' or 'forms of being' in the meanings set out above, and, if we are honest, we have to admit to finding it hard to enter into the minds of those who thought as the fourth-century philosophers thought – unless we are professional historians of philosophy. So the phrase 'of one being with the Father' may seem to us, in spite of all that can be said about it, to be a sounding brass or a tinkling cymbal.

But we do well to notice one thing about it. The divine essence is plainly neither male nor female – such words are inappropriate to the being of God. If, as the Creed says, the essence of Christ is the essence also of the father, there can be no question of ascribing maleness to Christ within the community of the Trinity. The Creed certainly gives no ground for supposing that either the Father or the Son is a male person; it is the later depictions both of the Father (which are rare) and of the Son (which are common) as glorified *men* in ecclesiastical art, which have given rise to this false idea. This truth, at least, the obscure terminology of the Creed makes clear.

All this is certainly a far cry from Jesus as we know him in the Gospels. Yet perhaps it is easier now to see that to do justice to this same Jesus whom now we worship as Son of God, after his resurrection and in the light of his achievements and power in the past and in the present, a stupendous effort of thinking has been and still is required of his church. The creeds are the early fruits of this effort which still goes on. Meanwhile, however, we may be content to say of Christ that he has the full authority of God the Father for what he does and says and is, that his work in salvation is the work also of the Father, and that he and the Father – and, as we shall see, the Holy Spirit – are eternally linked in a relationship which no words of ours can describe. Augustine, who did much fruitful thinking about the Trinity, said at the end: 'We speak (only) that we may not remain silent'; and, 'All things go away into mystery'.

Almost as an afterthought, the Creed adds: '*Through him all things were made.*' We are back to scriptural language again with some relief; this is virtually a quotation from John's Gospel (1.3): 'Through him [i.e. the Word] all things came to be; no single thing was created without him.' And it agrees with the Letter to the Colossians (written by Paul or another) (1.16): 'The whole universe has been created through him and for him.'

Here again, in Scripture and in Creed, the language has to be taken as mythological. We are not asked to imagine that when God the Father, maker of heaven and earth, and of all things, seen and unseen, was engaged in his work of creation, God the Son literally stood by his side and said the creative words in unison with him. We are being told, and invited to believe, that the work of creation (which, as we have already seen, still goes on) is the work of God, Father, Son and Holy Spirit (for the Holy Spirit is the 'giver of life'), one God; and this means that the principle of love which to us is most clearly seen in Christ underlies the whole creative activity of God. And this scotches the idea which is still to be found even among Christians that some parts of the universe are neutral, or even evil, and reaffirms the statement of Genesis, that 'God saw all that he had made, and it was very good' (1.31).

Much of this chapter has been, unavoidably, high up in the clouds. It is time to come down to earth, as Christ himself did.

4 *For us men and for our salvation he came down from heaven, and was made man. . . .*

The Christian faith as it has been understood until now stands or falls by the truth or otherwise of the doctrine of the Incarnation – that Jesus Christ, the eternal Son of the Father, became man and lived and died on earth.

The passages in the New Testament which affirm this teaching are statements of historical fact, for without historical facts there would be no case for believing in the Incarnation. At the same time these passages are mythological, for the import of such an astonishing doctrine can be conveyed only in the form of myth. It is sometimes hard to be sure what is history and what is myth.

So we have: 'The Word became flesh; he came to dwell among us, and we saw his glory, such glory as befits the Father's only son, full of grace and truth' (John 1.14); 'God loved the world so much that he gave his only Son, that everyone who has faith in him may not die but have eternal life' (John 3.16); 'You know how generous our Lord Jesus Christ has been: he was rich, yet for your sake he became poor, so that through his poverty you might become rich' (II Cor. 8.9); 'For the divine nature was his from the first; yet he did not think to snatch at equality with God, but made himself nothing, assuming the nature of a slave' (Phil. 2.6–7).

The Creed goes to the heart of these and other passages, and by a succession of short phrases drives home the faith of the Incarnation. *'For us men and for our salvation, he came down from heaven.'* This is not the narrative of an 'upstairs, downstairs' event, how one of 'them' came to visit his inferiors; nor does it describe a movement from one area of space to another. It tells us straight out that Jesus Christ exchanged the joys of heaven, that is the immediate presence of God the Father, for the chequered existence of human beings on earth and shared it to the full as 'one of us'.

It is unfortunate that modern translations of the Creed still retain the word 'men' in this clause. The plain meaning is, of course, 'human beings', but in the past many Christians (though perhaps no one at present) have supposed that it was for the salvation of male human beings that Christ came, and that women are saved, not directly by Christ, but through the mediation of their menfolk. Presumably the word 'men' was sometimes misunderstood in this sense, though the reasons for the mistake lie deeper, in the traditional relationships between women and men and in the sense of male superiority that for a long time was fostered by the church.

It was for us that he came. This can only mean that the motive for his coming was love of the human race – 'God loved the world so much'. This is not explicitly stated in the terse language of the Creed, and was perhaps not uppermost in the minds of those who wrote it; but the repetition later on ('on *our behalf* he was crucified') shows that they were not unaware of it. In our thinking and teaching we must bring it right out into the open, for there is no other motive which is able to explain why Christ did what he did.

When we read the word 'salvation' we are inclined to think at once of the salvation of our *souls*. But this does the Creed an injustice. The New Testament speaks of the salvation of whole persons, not just of their 'souls' (a word which presumably means their spiritual parts, though this is not a biblical idea). Again, we limit 'salvation' to the forgiveness of our sins, and the giving of new life in Christ – and these are important parts of it; but the Christians at the Councils must certainly have included the enlightenment of our minds; indeed some of the fathers of the church can be justly charged with placing the enlightenment of our minds above the forgiveness of our sins in importance. Both are included in 'salvation' – as well as much more besides. Education, for instance, is certainly included within the scope of 'salvation', for it is concerned with the whole process of personal growth. So is liberation from oppression, economic, racial and sexual.

Since the Renaissance and the Reformation we have come to think of salvation in purely personal terms, and have thus given hostages to those who for reasons of their own wish to 'keep religion out of politics'. It was the *world* that God loved so much; and the world is not just a collection of individuals but the whole complex of human society at every level. The salvation which God offers through Christ is not limited to you and me and every other individual inhabitant of the globe (though it *is* offered to each of us); it is offered to the *world*. This is the truth re-captured in whole or in part by 'Liberation Theology' which, quite rightly, includes all human society, economic, social, and political, within the scope of salvation – just as the Old Testament prophets did.

'*By the power of the Holy Spirit he became incarnate from the Virgin Mary, and was made man.*' The coming of Jesus, motivated by love, was enabled by the Holy Spirit, the giver of life. To try to say more about the 'why' and the 'how' of the Incarnation is to attempt to plumb the depths of God's mind, and it may be that the silence of the New Testament is a warning that the attempt should not be made. It is hard to restrain human speculation on the matter, but in this instance it does not get us very far.

'*By the Virgin Mary*'. It cannot be said too strongly or too often that birth from the Virgin Mary is adduced in the Creed *not* to indicate the divine method of bringing about the Incarnation (that matter is sufficiently covered by the phrase 'the power of the Holy Spirit'), but, most certainly, to demonstrate the *human* origin of the incarnate Christ. No doubt the bishops at the Council (though, as we know, not all bishops at the present time) all believed that Jesus was virginally conceived by Mary, for this belief was by this time part of the received tradition of the church. But they did not refer to Mary's virginity in order to prove Christ's deity; they are saying, rather, that the coming of Jesus through the processes of human birth in the womb of Mary demonstrates his humanity; they are repeating the point made by Paul (in Gal. 4.4), 'God sent his own Son, born of a woman, born under the law'. It is not on the virginity but on the humanity of Mary that they lay their stress.

But what are we ourselves to think about the Virgin Birth, which is an obstacle to many people's faith? Neither Paul nor John, the principal exponents of the Incarnation in the New Testament, make any mention of a Virgin Birth of Jesus. Perhaps they had never been told that it had happened; certainly they built their teaching of the Incarnation most carefully without any reference to it whatsoever. It cannot, therefore, be necessary for us to assert the Virgin Birth in order to have a full doctrine of the Incarnation. We do not reject the truth which the phrase in the Creed about the Virgin Mary is intended to convey if we deny or doubt the historical occurrence of the Virgin Birth. Whether it did occur or not, whether it is fact or myth, perhaps we can never know; all we can do is assess the evidence and make up our minds.

So far as evidence is concerned, the Gospels of Matthew and Luke definitely assert the historicity of the Virgin Birth, though in passages widely believed to be of a 'folklore' character, very different from the rest of their gospels; the remainder of the New Testament is silent on the matter. The evidence, clearly, is inconclusive – surely not strong enough on the traditional side to assert unreservedly that it really happened.

'*Incarnate*'. The word in itself simply means 'made flesh', that is born as a human baby, though in Christian usage it has come to include the whole range of Christ's life and character on earth. Here we have it in its original sense: Jesus Christ was born of Mary in a human body of flesh and blood.

'*And was made man*'. The climax of the paragraph, and of the whole statement of the doctrine of the Incarnation comes exactly here. Perhaps '*became* man' would be a more exact translation. 'Man' of course is again used to mean 'human being'; the essence of the Incarnation is that he became a human being, not that he became a male person, though as a human being he plainly had to be of one sex or the other, and was, in fact, male. If he had become a woman the history of the world might have been different. But in the conditions of the time this possibility had to be ruled out.

In the years that followed the Council of Constantinople the theological arguments in the church (the Christians of that time were incurably argumentative) centred on this phrase. The relation between the Son and the Father had now been settled by the Councils (at least for the time being). But how on earth (literally) could Christ be both divine and human at the same time, as the Nicene Creed had certainly affirmed that he was?

Speculation on this matter had indeed been rife even before the Council of Constantinople, and the idea had been floated that the incarnate Christ had a human body but a divine centre of personality. But this made nonsense of his claim to be human; for the centre of personality is surely the prime element in a human life. After the Council, in accordance with current ways of thinking about human beings, it was held that in the incarnate Christ there was something called 'human nature' – which we all have – and something called 'divine nature' – which only Christ had. But how could they both be in the same person? Some said they simply coexisted side by side in Christ, and that sometimes the human nature was at work, as when he had a meal, and sometimes the divine nature, as when he performed a miracle. This was a kind of Cox and Box theory, which almost made him out to be two persons, perhaps even schizophrenic. Others said that the two natures were *united* in him. It was at first objected that this would have to mean that the divine was dominant and the human nature subordinate, for in a union between the divine and the human the divine was bound to prevail. But the objection was overruled, and the Council of Chalcedon in 451 came down firmly in favour of this second view, though it did insist that the Incarnate Christ was truly man as well as truly God, and that he was 'in all things like us, without sin'. (See for this, and further complexities, the Chalcedonian Definition on p. 88.)

The problem was plainly not solved. The effect of the prolonged discussions and the decision at Chalcedon was, as we can now see more clearly by hindsight than anyone at the time could have been expected to see, definitely to emphasize the deity of Christ at the expense of his humanity. And Christian art down the centuries bears eloquent testimony to this. The authentic teaching of the church that Christ on earth is our example was seriously endangered, and has been in danger ever since. If Christ, though asserted to be human as well as divine, was preserved from sinning by his divine nature – as Christian piety has often implied – what use is he to us, who experience the fierceness of temptation without a built-in safeguard against giving way to it? Some people have even said that his human nature was impersonal; but this makes no sense at all.

In modern times, therefore, there have been many attempts to restore the humanity of Christ in books and teaching about him; sometimes, even, people have revived the ancient theory that he was a very good man elevated to deity because of the purity of his life – that he rose from the ranks and was promoted to Son of God, at his baptism or through his resurrection. This theory was summarily rejected by several councils of the church even before Nicaea, on the ground that if he was a man who became God he cannot be the eternal Son of the Father, a doctrine that lay at the heart of Christianity.

It may be that the time has now come to grasp the nettle and take the phrase 'he became man' with *complete seriousness*, without even the reservation that at a pinch he could always call for supernatural help. If we take this approach, then Jesus was, quite simply, a man – a man with superb gifts of mind and spirit, a man in close communion with his Father in heaven, but a man. He lived as one of us; he was subject to the limitations of human knowledge and understanding, and to the temptation native to the human condition, and to the hardships and joys which come to all of us in large or small measure. It was as a man that he performed the surprising acts which we call 'miracles', some of which have been heightened (hyped?) in our records to show how 'divine' he was; it was as a man that he made plain the love of God and followed the way of love to the bitter end.

If so, *this* was the way that the divine Son of God chose to reveal the love of God, to fulfil his mission and to offer salvation to the world; and it was his faithfulness, courage and endurance in following this way that God the Father honoured and accepted by raising him from the dead. Of course, a terrible risk had been taken: but we have seen already that the motive of the Incarnation was love for the human race, and love, by its very nature and intention, is prepared to take risks, even the greatest ones.

There are objections to this view which will occur to the reader. Does it really account for the miracles? Do we know enough about his life to make the necessary claims? But there are also many objections to every other view that has been put forward. This one can be a step forward in the exploration of 'the mystery of the Incarnation' which must still go on, and which the Nicene Creed and the Chalcedonian Definition did not bring to an end.

It can be put in this way:

> God's Word, through ages spoken,
> By prophet, deed and token,
> Into our life has broken
> In person of a man.
> His makeshift crib a manger,
> To easy life a stranger,
> Inured to constant danger,
> He bodied forth God's plan.
>
> In father and in mother,
> In sister and in brother,

In care of one another,
The love of God he traced.
He saw in pride of nation,
In women's subjugation,
In racial domination,
God's image gone to waste.

The dispossessed acclaimed him,
The 'king' and 'saviour' named him;
The powerful defamed him,
With blind injustice slew.
From death released, ascending,
Race, sex and class transcending,
He lives, in love contending,
The Word of God come true.

(R.E.D.)

'*For our sake he was crucified under Pontius Pilate; he suffered death and was buried.*' There is no doubt about the facts of his crucifixion, death and burial. These are real events in history, and their recital is necessary for the full statement of the Incarnation; indeed it is a pity that more known historical facts are not recited – we miss all reference to his youth and manhood, his teaching, his character and his power. The account of his earthly life and death is slightly out of joint, and we must fill it out by our own knowledge as we say the Creed.

(The Apostles' Creed has something at this point which was discarded at Nicaea and Constantinople: 'He descended into hell.' We should more correctly say: 'He descended into *Hades*', this being the place into which we all go at death according to the later books of the Old Testament. The clause seems to be based on the passage in the First Epistle of Peter according to which 'Christ preached to the spirits in prison' (3.19), in the period between the crucifix-

ion and the resurrection. This whole idea can be said to
indicate, by way of a myth, that Jesus died and was raised
from the dead to save not only the people who lived in his
own time and afterwards, but also those who had died
before he came – and, we may safely say, those who have
lived since his time without the knowledge of his coming. It
is, then, best understood as a myth of the universal love of
Christ.)

All this was 'for our sake'. The bishops in the councils
were very wise not to set out an exact doctrine of the way in
which Christ atoned for our sins. To 'atone' is to 'reconcile'
us with God, and the New Testament clearly says that he
did that. But there is no explicit doctrine about this in the
New Testament, though many people have read several
such doctrines into it – and sometimes made one or other of
them into a party cry. What we have is a number of vivid
pictures, each of which throws light on the 'atoning work'
of Jesus on the cross. So we read that he came to 'give up his
life as a ransom for many' (Mark 10.45); that he 'was
innocent of sin, and yet for our sake God made him one
with the sinfulness of men, so that in him we might be
made one with his goodness' (II Cor. 5.21); that 'if we walk
in the light . . . we are being cleansed from our sin by the
blood of God's Son' (I John 1.7); that God 'designed him to
be the means of expiating sin by his sacrificial death' (Rom.
3.25); and that on the cross Christ encountered and
defeated the demonic powers that prey on human life (Col.
2.15) and 'made peace through the shedding of his blood
upon the cross' (Col. 1.20). These are all striking images of
the effect of Christ's death, and images especially meaning-
ful to those who had lived within the sacrificial systems of
the ancient world; but they are images only, striking
though they are. There is no hint anywhere that Christ died
to appease (or 'propitiate') an angry God (though some of

the older translations seem to suggest as much), or that Christ substituted for us by enduring the punishment that we deserve. The emphasis everywhere is on the love of God, Father and Son, for the human race in its sad plight. 'God was in Christ reconciling the world to himself, no longer holding men's misdeeds against them' (II Cor. 5.19).

We can, then, say this: we, and all other members of the human race, are sinful people, and our sins, repeated in every age, brought Jesus to the cross. He did not respond, as he had the right to do, by inflicting on us the punishment that we deserve. On the contrary, he offered his forgiveness, and that offer has the seal of God upon it. If we accept it, we are reconciled to God.

'*On the third day he rose again*'. The narratives of the resurrection of Christ (of which Paul's in I Cor. 15 is by far the earliest) are hard, even impossible, to harmonize with each other. But they are agreed on one point – Jesus Christ after his death was once again alive, in contact with his friends, active in the world, and promising his presence with his friends until the end of time; and this was God's doing, for our benefit in this world and the next. This is the heart of the matter, and, beside it, questions about the *mode* of his resurrection – whether his body was removed by God from his tomb, or whether he was personally present with his disciples in a non-physical, entirely new way – fade into insignificance. He was alive, he *is* alive. This is what really matters.

On the matter of the 'empty tomb', however, it should be said that whereas the gospels all speak of the disappearance of his body from the tomb, there is no trace of such a statement in Paul's writings. What is quite certain is that Paul constructed his theological ideas about life in Christ, and about our personal resurrection, without any reference to an empty tomb; and so we, presumably, are at liberty to assert or deny the emptiness of the tomb, according to the way in which we evaluate the evidence, without touching any really vital issues.

'*In accordance with the scriptures*'. No one since the time of the councils has been able to tell us for sure which scriptures the Creed has in mind. Probably, like Paul, when he made a similar statement (I. Cor. 15.4), it refers to the scriptures of the Old Testament which were thought to foretell the resurrection of Christ. But, in this case, *which* scriptures? 'After two days he will revive us, on the third day he will restore us, that we may live in his presence' says Hosea (6.2), the prophet of the eighth century BC. This may have been taken by the early Christians to be a foreshadowing of the life of the Messiah (they used a collection of such passages in their teaching), and so was readily applied to Jesus. Or, just possibly, the clause may refer to the Christian scriptures which the Council of Nicaea had authorized and arranged in what we call 'the Canon of Scripture'.

'*He ascended into heaven and is seated on the right hand of the Father.*' We must certainly understand this clause as a myth, and as an especially valuable myth. We cannot believe, except by a sheer effort of irrational will, that Jesus literally 'went up' to heaven forty days after the resurrection; nor can we stomach the idea that he is now literally seated in a particular place; or that heaven is a place at all. But it *is* a Christian conviction, founded on scripture and tested in the experience of the church, personal and corporate, that the time came when Jesus no longer appeared in person to the disciples in the limited area of Palestine, and became available to all people everywhere in the world. This is the conviction attested by the story of the Ascension.

It is also a Christian conviction that Jesus has been 'exalted' and 'glorified' by his crucifixion and resurrection. Having fulfilled his mission on earth, he has cast off his earthly limitations, worthy now of even greater worship than before, and, more importantly still, incorporating us into the renewed humanity of which he is the pioneer. This also is something of what is conveyed pictorially by the 'ascent into heaven', and still more by his 'sitting at the right hand of the Father'.

The glorified Christ has not lost his concern for human sins and sorrows, but since he is the new humanity, male and female, in his own person, he has transcended the difference of sex to which he was subject during his incarnation. He is the 'new person' – not the 'new *man*' or the 'new *woman*'. It follows that the ordained priesthood which represents on earth the 'great High Priest' in heaven must consist of both men and women, if it is not to be hopelessly inadequate for its task. To think of the risen and ascended Christ as still male is to impoverish, very seriously, our view of him and our conception of the Christian ministry.

'He will come again in glory to judge the living and the dead'. The early Christians believed so vividly in the 'Second Coming' that they could not imagine that it would be long delayed. The Fathers of Nicaea and Constantinople had to reckon with his non-arrival – so far. But they assert that he *will* come – in his own time, we must add, not ours, and not in any time that we can predict, even by careful study of the scriptures or of the internal measurement of the pyramids.

Here, surely, we are still in the realm of powerful myth – the myth which points to the final divine judgment on human history.

Some Christians, however, still prefer to take the promise of his coming quite literally, and expect that Christ will be seen with the physical human eye, riding on the clouds of glory. But let it be said that this is to rob the language of its force. If we take it literally, we are tied down to consideration of the physical details – for instance, where on earth, if anywhere, will it be possible for everyone to see him in the sky? But if we see the poetry in the words, we are able to receive the penetrating truth that all human people and all human activities stand under the judgment of Christ, who will declare his verdict when the time for that has come.

The prospect of a definitive judgment either at death or on the Day of Judgment fills many people with terror, especially those with a temperament prone to guilty feelings, or an upbringing which has encouraged these, and the church in some ages has not been slow to exploit this fact, either with the bad motive of frightening people into obedience or with the better motive of persuading them to repent and be saved. But the terror is unjustified, and the exploitation unjustifiable. 'We believe that he will come to be our judge', says the Te Deum, echoing the Creed. It is Jesus who will come – the Jesus whom we know, not a Jesus changed out of all recognition into a fierce avenger. Evil deeds not repented of must of course be judged; but Jesus 'desires not the death of a sinner, but rather that he should turn from his wickedness and live'. The mercy of Jesus lasts unless and until we ourselves finally reject it.

'*And his kingdom will have no end*'. For a moment the Creed looks beyond the pains and persecutions, the happiness and successes, the griefs and the failures, the good deeds of charity and the evil deeds of selfishness, the ever-present readiness of human societies to condone their own wickedness and to condemn that of others, the signs of progress sometimes, the signs of retrogression more often seen – beyond all these into the eternal reign of Christ which takes over when the present age is finished, judged, and gone. But the promise of this magnificent future is not inserted in order to dull us to the needs of the present world as we contemplate the satisfactions of the future. On the contrary, if the gospels are to be trusted, Christ inaugurated God's kingdom, which is also his kingdom, while he was on earth, and called and equipped his followers in his church to live as members of that kingdom from that moment on, and to take every possible step to make it real there and then in human society. This denies Christians the easy option of otherworldliness, and places them in the forefront of the struggle for justice and peace.

Which brings us to the Holy Spirit, the Lord and Life-giver.

5 The Holy Spirit, the Lord, the Giver of Life, who proceeds from the Father and the Son. . .

'*We believe in the Holy Spirit*'. The Christian church in all its parts and at all times has found it very difficult to get its mind clear on the subject of the Holy Spirit. No one has ever doubted the Holy Spirit's existence, though sometimes he has been regarded simply as a kind of 'influence' exerted by Jesus Christ ('the Spirit of Jesus'); but every formulation of his nature and his activities so far produced turns out to be vague and indeterminate, and only very few people would say that the sermons they had heard, or had given, on the subject were particularly illuminating.

Why is this? One reason may be that the Holy Spirit's activities are normally unobtrusive. The creative works of God the Father are manifest in nature; and he occupies a large place in the teaching of Jesus. Jesus Christ the Son has deliberately made himself known in visible and unmistakeable form, so that we can see 'the glory of God in the face of Jesus Christ'. But the Holy Spirit works silently and invisibly, in the processes of history, the life of the church and the inner recesses of the human mind. He does not make himself prominent, as the Father and the Son need to make themselves prominent.

But a stronger reason is that the Holy Spirit is above all

the innovative, the incalculable, the unpredictable Person in the Trinity. Of course, the Trinity has all these qualities, and so has each Person of the Trinity. The creation is always liable to burst out in something we did not expect, especially in human personality. And here is the Spirit's special role.

The life and death and teaching of Christ, and his presence in his church, may at any time lead us into unexpected depths of experience and on to unexpected heights. But in the ordinary run of things, in our ordinary worship and our day-to-day activities, we know what to expect of nature, of ourselves, and of the processes of thought in which we engage when we are thinking about the Father and the Son. Prayers and sermons and books on religion and theology tend to follow a predictable pattern (except on rare occasions). Nor is this in itself a bad thing; for the human self and the human community need a reliable background against which to deal with the changes which crowd in upon us every day – and in modern conditions almost every minute.

The Holy Spirit (we can just as well call the Holy Spirit 'she', for the word in Hebrew is feminine, in Greek neuter and in Latin masculine – and to use the neuter pronoun would obscure the personhood) is co-responsible with the Father and the Son for creation and with the Son and the Father in bringing about our salvation (the doctrine of the Trinity becomes very complex at this point!); but he (we say 'he', because of general usage) is not content to allow us simply to settle down with a well-worked-out system of thought or scheme of practical living. He does not wish us to settle down at all. He is for ever waking us up out of our complacency and causing us to question our prejudices and our presuppositions. There is no statutory age for us to stop thinking or understanding new ideas.

Now this is very disturbing for the church, and every section of it, when it has worked out its doctrines and enshrined them in creeds and constitutions and laws. 'This has all been settled; why trouble us?', it says, and resists the change suggested. Indeed many, perhaps most, of the crises and conflicts in the history of the church from the beginning have been caused by the unwillingness of the church to accept or welcome a new idea, or a new practice, that was likely to disrupt its institutional life. Without this unwillingness, the Reformation and the separation of Methodism from the Church of England would never have happened, and there might now be a united church in this country. This does not suggest that all proposed changes are Spirit-inspired; but it explains why so many good changes have been resisted and avoided.

If the Spirit behaves in this way, it is hard to pin him down by definitions, doctrines and credal statements. Hence the vagueness of 'pneumatic' doctrine (i.e. doctrine about the Spirit). On the one hand the theologians of the church have rightly said that the Spirit eludes our definitions, and that therefore it is best to say little. On the other hand, not so rightly, they have been reluctant to give him a title which describes his innovative activity, lest too many innovations are thereby justified and shatter the established order of church life and thought.

Hence also the rather drab statement about the Holy Spirit in the Nicene Creed:

'The Lord'. To the Holy Spirit, as to Jesus Christ, is ascribed the highest possible title – but a title given to him only after long controversy. *'The Giver of Life'*. The life which he gives is in the first place the natural life of all created beings, and in the second place the 'new' life which is offered to us through faith in Christ. There have always been Christians, and may be some still, who believe that the

life-giving activities of the Spirit did not begin until he was sent by Jesus Christ into the world and into the hearts of the disciples at his own departure (John 14.16; and there is some ground for this view in John 7.39), except that by a special, anticipatory, provision he inspired the writers of the Old Testament. But, in that case, what was the source of truth and goodness in those who built up societies of the human race on principles of justice and honesty (after all, it was the Greeks, not Christians, who invented democracy), or in those poets, artists, philosophers and teachers of the ancient world whose wisdom we still accept and treasure? Without Socrates, Plato, Aristotle, Sophocles and Euripides we should certainly lack much of what we call Christian culture. And, by a parallel argument, what is the source of the revelations of truth which we owe to other faiths which have little or no knowledge of Christ? It is more in accord with the general tenor of Old Testament and New Testament teaching, and not least with the firm biblical tradition that the Holy Spirit, often thought of as wisdom personified, was present with the Father at creation, and it is at the same time more consistent with the generosity of God, to suppose that the Holy Spirit has at all times inspired, influenced and co-operated with (whatever words we may choose to use) people of every time and race whose prime concern was the pursuit of truth and goodness. If this is sound, then we can trace the activities of the creator Spirit in every human society, in every religious faith and every system of thought; for not one has been entirely devoid of everything good. We can trace them more clearly in the art and literature of the classical world, and in the thinkers and teachers and constructive statesmen not only of Israel but also of Greece and Rome. It may be that the reason why we cannot trace them so clearly elsewhere is just that we are still largely ignorant of these cultures.

This, and much more, is the work of the Holy Spirit in the world; indeed there is no end in sight to his life-giving in this comprehensive sense. Moreover, in many ways and places he has prepared people and communities for the coming of Jesus Christ by giving them a knowledge of God on which the insights of Christianity can build.

His activities in the fellowship of Christian believers are more obvious, just as Christian refusal to accept his guidance is also more obvious. He forever gives new life to the whole body of the church; indeed, one of the church's leading characteristics, as we are reminded every time we say or hear the Benediction, is 'the fellowship of the Holy Spirit', which would be much better translated by '*sharing in* the Holy Spirit', that is, in the life and power which he gives.

It is true, but not always noticed, that the New Testament has much more to say about the Holy Spirit at work in the community than about his empowerment of individual people, from the Day of Pentecost onwards; and that fact is especially relevant today when the individual appropriation of the Holy Spirit's gifts, so long neglected, is being so heavily stressed. The pendulum has swung in this direction throughout many Christian circles, and the constant effort of the Holy Spirit to bind the Christian community into one body is being devalued, in order, as it sometimes seems, to provide a kind of excuse for the failure of the churches to unite with each other. In this new climate we have a contrast between those who claim for themselves the individual 'gifts' of the Spirit and those who value more highly the 'fruits' of the Spirit, a contrast which often degenerates into a competition between the 'charismatics' and those who maintain the orderly life of the church. The former claim the 'gifts' of the Spirit, the latter speak more about the 'fruits'.

But both the 'gifts' and the 'fruits' belong to the unity of the whole church, and if they disrupt this they are not genuine gifts or fruits of the Spirit at all. The fruits, or more properly the fruit, the harvest, of the Spirit – love, joy, peace, patience, kindness, goodness, fidelity, gentleness, and self-control – are a gift of the Spirit; and love, says Paul, is its principal component. Without this harvest of the Spirit, this treasury of gifts, or at least without growth towards it, there is no new life in the church. The other gifts are useless without it, and can do positive harm if arrogance, not love, stirs up the brew.

But the other gifts are important also, not chiefly for the well-being and happiness of the individual (though this is not insignificant), but chiefly for the building up of the church. The Greek word for them that Paul uses, *charisma*, has nowadays, rather surprisingly, come into common use in a confusing variety of meanings. For Paul the essential ingredient of the word is '*grace*' (charis) – the free, undeserved generosity of God, the Holy Spirit; the gifts spring from grace. And one or more gifts is offered to every person without exception; there is no hint that the 'extraordinary' gifts (such as that of 'tongues') are of any more value for their purpose than the more humdrum ones of teaching and administration (indeed, Paul tends to downgrade the gift of 'speaking with tongues', in comparison with 'clear speaking').

The new life given by the Spirit is, as we know, nourished by prayer, sacraments and the common life in fellowship. These (apart from, briefly, the sacrament of baptism) are not mentioned in the Creed, presumably because they were not yet the subjects of controversy – as they later became. The virtual absence of sacramental doctrine certainly impairs the wholeness of the Creed. It is just as well, therefore, that it is used more frequently in the context of

eucharistic worship than on any other occasion, since we
are then reminded that the creativity and fatherhood of
God, the redemptive work of the Son and the life-giving
action of the Spirit, which are rehearsed in most liturgies
in the Great Prayer of Thanksgiving, are embodied and
made available to us in the eucharist; and in the same act
of worship, corporate and individual prayers are offered,
and the common life of fellowship is manifested. So the
omissions of the Creed are to this extent repaired.

'Who proceeds from the Father and the Son'. There is no
clause in the Creed, surely, which is repeated with greater
incomprehension by ministers and people than this one!
At this point the Creed makes a further excursion, rather
imprudently, into the inner life of God, the Three in One;
and it does not emerge unscathed. But we must try to see
what the writers were getting at. They were agreed (after a
long controversy in the years before the Council of Constantinople), that the Spirit is 'of one Being with the
Father' (*homoousios* – that fatal word), as is the Son. But
how is the relation of the Spirit to the Father within the
community of the Trinity to be described? The relationship
of Jesus Christ with the Father, they had already said, is
most truly put as the relationship between a son and a
father. But they thought that the case of the Spirit was
different. The notion that they came up with was 'procession' (not in our sense of the word) – the Spirit, they
decided, *proceeds from*, comes out from, the Father; that is
to say, his being has its origin in the being of the Father,
and it is in fact the same being, though the *persons* of
Father and Spirit are distinct. The Spirit is not subordinate
to the Father, any more than the Son is subordinate to the
Father, for his proceeding from the Father is not something which happened once for all on an occasion in the
distant past, so that there was a time when the Spirit did

not exist; *the procession is eternal, timeless*, and the Spirit also is eternal, timeless.

This reasoning is subtle and esoteric; modern ways of thinking may not ever come to terms with it, and we are surely tempted to leave it on one side. A little light may begin to dawn on us, however, when we are told that there is a second meaning of 'procession' – that the Spirit is *sent out by* the Father. A famous description of the Spirit in early times calls him 'one of the two hands of God' – Jesus being the other hand. The Spirit and the Son are the agents by which God is at work in the world. This may be helpful, but 'hands' are impersonal (as we depersonalize industrial workers by calling them 'hands'); and we do better to call the Spirit and the Son 'God's partners and agents in the world' – partners, we might say, in a close-knit but outward-looking family unit whose bond is love, among themselves and for those whom they serve.

Fortunately, we can know the Spirit for ourselves, and *in* ourselves and others, without grasping the intangible mysteries of his eternal being, as yet so imperfectly and obscurely worked out by the church!

But a further conflict looms up. The Nicene Creed said in 381 that the Spirit 'proceeds from the Father', and makes no reference to the Son in relation to the Spirit. After the promulgation of the Creed, many people came to think that the Son ought to have been mentioned (or else he might feel insulted?), and canvassed the possible statement that the Spirit 'proceeds from the Father through the Son'. This was popular in the churches of the Western Roman Empire under the influence of Augustine of Hippo, perhaps the greatest single force in Western Christianity since the time of the apostles. At least it did more justice to Jesus' sending of the Spirit into the world. Later, Augustine's supporters came to favour a simpler reference to the Son, made by adding to the clause about the Spirit the phrase 'and the Son'. As this was known at first only to the churches where Latin was spoken, the phrase came to be called 'the filioque clause'. Those who used it felt strongly that the short clause in the Nicene Creed did not give sufficient honour to Jesus Christ; and that the addition did not make any real difference to what was affirmed about the Spirit.

So far, no doubt, the difference of opinion was natural and legitimate. But political factors soon began to play an ugly role. The provinces in the Eastern Roman Empire became more and more separate, for political and military reasons, from those in the Western Empire; and in the tumultuous conditions of what we call the Dark Ages, when communications from country to country almost disappeared, the churches of East and West became separate too. Rivalries between the bishops in the East and the bishops in the West, fuelled by Eastern repugnance to the claims of the Bishop of Rome, bedevilled the issue. When it was known in the East that Roman monks were singing the filioque in the liturgical use of the Creed, a serious *casus belli* was provided for those who wished to make use of it, and those were many. The cry was raised that the so-called Christians of the West had tampered with the Creed and become heretical, while the East had remained loyal to the true faith, and could now alone be styled 'orthodox'.

Charlemagne, king of the Franks, liberator of Christian Europe from the Muslims, and, under the title of Holy Roman Emperor from 800, restorer of the ancient dignity, unity and culture of the Western Empire, instructed the Pope to slip the filioque into the Creed; it had been so long accepted in the churches which he knew about that it seemed the natural thing to do. The Pope refused; but his successors allowed it to happen. When the news of this outrage reached the Patriarch of Constantinople, the fuse was set for the final breach between East and West. The date for this is usually given as 1054; complete breaches of communion had taken place before this, and had been outwardly healed. The claims of the Papacy, and the permission to marry given to Eastern clergy, and not to their Western brethren, had joined with the filioque controversy to produce a series of complex conflicts; but underneath all this was a struggle for power over the minds and loyalties of (allegedly) fellow-Christians. In the end nobody won, and each side claimed the victory.

The doctrinal issue was never quite absent from the imbroglio, and now that the noise of battle has died away, it is the main matter of disagreement between the Orthodox churches of the East on the one hand, and the churches of the West, both those which acknowledge the supremacy of the Pope and those which have rebelled against it, on the other hand. The Orthodox churches, however, have played a full part in the World Council of Churches for some time; and as a gesture of reconciliation the present Archbishop of Canterbury arranged for the omission of the filioque from his service of Enthronement, in view of the presence at that service of an Orthodox dignitary. But while the filioque remains in the Nicene Creed as it is recited in the West, and the Orthodox refuse to countenance it, there can be no complete unity between the Orthodox and the other great Christian churches.

'*With the Father and the Son he is worshipped and glorified.*' We turn with some relief to less controversial matters, and ascribe to the Spirit the worship and glory which we ascribe to the Father and to the Son.

'*He has spoken through the Prophets.*' This is the second reference to the scriptures in the Creed. Christ 'rose again in accordance with the Scriptures'; and now this. This reference also is probably to the Old Testament (though the 'prophets' in mind *may* be the inspired preachers called 'prophets' in the New Testament, of which the four daughters of Philip (Acts 21.9) are striking examples; but this is unlikely), and shows how important a place the Old Testament held in the life of the early church. In particular, as is indicated both here and in the first reference, the Christians of the time believed that the Old Testament prophets, inspired by the Holy Spirit, had foretold both the coming of Jesus and the details of his life, death and resurrection.

This is difficult for us, because a close study of the prophetic passages in question by modern analytic methods shows that they frequently do not, on any honest interpretation, say what they have been traditionally thought to say; for instance, Isaiah did not write 'a virgin shall conceive and bear a son', but 'a young woman shall conceive and bear a son' (7.14). And when the prophetic words do seem to operate nicely as a description of coming events, they usually have to be taken out of their context in order for this to be so. The greatest difficulty of all lies in the notion that the actions of people in the far future are so exactly predetermined that they can be described in advance. If the sufferings of Jesus were really foretold in detail, and therefore predetermined, hundreds of years before, is not the guilt of those who betrayed and murdered him removed by the fact that they could not have done otherwise?

We are bound therefore to suppose that when the Spirit 'spoke by the prophets' he was not enabling them to perform an act of soothsaying. What he was doing, surely, was to inspire them to see more clearly than their contemporaries the deeper implications of God's dealings in history with the Jewish people, and of the situation in which they and their fellow-countrypeople found themselves. Jesus, well versed in the scriptures, and especially in the prophetic writings, was able to identify himself with the most perceptive thoughts of the prophets who preceded him. He proceeded to embody, develop, and fulfil them in his obedience to the will of his father. He did this most conspicuously in the case of 'the suffering servant of God', who is depicted by the Second Isaiah. The prophet did not have the Messiah in mind, but his vision sprang from a profound insight into the will of God.

Thus we are not tied by the clause in the Creed to a view of the literal infallibility of the prophetic books, or to any view of inspiration which does not stand up to fair enquiry. On the contrary, we can freely assert that the Spirit 'spoke by the prophets', and can make that assertion without compromising any of the established principles of biblical criticism – which themselves can well be ascribed to the guidance of the Holy Spirit, in view of the light which they have thrown on the meaning of scripture.

The clause, however, refers only to the past, and, for us, to the very distant past. Can we say that the Spirit still speaks 'by the prophets'? It must be possible for us to say this, and to say it with confidence, since otherwise how can it be true that the Spirit is guiding us into all the truth, as Jesus in John promises that his disciples will be guided? The name 'prophet' is no doubt easily acquired (even dishonestly acquired), or given. The church has to decide, as it has had to decide in every age, who are true prophets and who are false; and how much of what the true prophets say is in itself true. This difficult decision is not reached by simply looking back to the documents which the church has canonized, and resisting any change which cannot be harmonized with them. Nor can it be done properly by any one denomination or group of denominations, except provisionally for its own purposes. No denomination can claim to have preserved the truths committed to it so faithfully, or to have discerned the truths granted to other denominations so clearly, that it can set itself up as the guardian and judge of the Spirit's guidance. This can be done, and the Spirit's guidance fully recognized and faithfully carried out, only by the united church of Christ – the one holy, catholic and apostolic church.

To this church we give our attention in the next chapter.

6 *One holy catholic and apostolic church – one baptism – the resurrection of the dead – the life of the world to come*

'*We believe in one holy catholic and apostolic church.*' We are not here just saying that a church is *probably* necessary, that it is a good idea for it to be one and not split up, and that on the whole holiness, catholicity and apostolicity (whatever they may mean) are no doubt desirable characteristics of the church. We are committing ourselves, as an article of faith, not only to the existence of the church, but also to its unity, catholicity and apostolicity. The trouble is that though no doubt the church does exist (with, nowadays, rather muzzy boundaries), it is not one, and it is not by any means in all respects holy, catholic and apostolic. You can maintain that the church is one only by identifying the church with the denomination to which you belong (as Roman Catholics used to do in the past, and certain Protestant sects still do) – which in our time is seen to be absurd. You can call it 'holy' only by shutting your eyes to the gross sins, and to the subtle ones, which are to be found in its history; and, in any case, the very fact that it is disunited shows that it is not really holy. You can claim catholicity for it only if you identify the whole faith with what your particular church holds, and that is a view which it becomes more and more difficult to take as we get to know what other churches believe (this point is taken up later). And to compare the modern church with that of the apostles, in the hope of finding that the church is 'apostolic', reveals some very obvious and painful discrepancies.

So what we are doing, in effect (it is a pity that we cannot do more), when we say this clause in the Creed, is committing ourselves to working and praying for the unity, holiness, catholicity and apostolicity of the church. Anyone, for instance, who says in worship that he or she believes in the unity of the church, and then proceeds to act or think – or just do nothing – in a way which makes unity more difficult to achieve than it is already, is breaking a commitment of faith which he or she has just made.

For the full import of all this to go home to us, we must be clear what unity and the other credally-blest characteristics really are. And before that can happen, we must know what the church is. The church is, clearly, the company of those who believe in Jesus Christ. But the New Testament says far more about it than that.

It describes the church in ninety-five different ways, each throwing light on some aspect of it. But the main descriptions of it are 'the body of Christ' and 'the people of God'. Those who call themselves 'Catholics' used to emphasize the former description, 'Protestants' the latter. But the difference of emphasis was unnecessary. The New Testament writers are just as natural and spontaneous when they speak of 'the body' as when they speak of 'the people', and the other way round. 'Body' indicates the corporate, organic nature of the Christian community. It is a very strong metaphor, pointing to the profound way in which Christians are linked together in the life given by Christ and the power given by the Spirit which they share with each other. In this context, Paul can say that if one member of the church suffers, then all the members suffer with him or her, and if one member is happy, then all the members share his or her happiness; and that the head of this body is Christ himself.

'The people of God' refers directly to God's new covenant with the church through Christ, and indirectly back to the 'ancient people of God', the Hebrew nation, with whom the original covenant was made by God through Moses. The church is the new 'covenanted people' of God. A 'people' is an assembly of persons who are brought together by a common origin, a common calling and a common purpose, who make decisions in common and proceed together to a common task when the decisions have been made. So the two descriptions fit well together.

Only slightly less important than the image of the church as the Body of Christ and the People of God is the image of the 'priesthood of all believers', the only human Christian priesthood mentioned in the New Testament. It is not that each of us individually is a priest, as good as any other priest, with the right of access to God which makes any intermediary superfluous. This is not the point of the description. The point is that *together* we constitute the corporate priesthood which continues the priestly ministry of Christ on earth, by representing humankind to God and God to humankind, offering prayers to God and preaching God's gospel to the world.

Since the church is the Body of Christ, the People of God and the priesthood of all believers, the meaning of unity is at once apparent. There cannot be more than one Body of Christ, more than one People of God, more than one priesthood of all believers, in the purpose of God; and if the church is divided up into churches, as it is, the purpose of God is being thwarted. This is a quite fundamental truth.

We cannot paper over the wide cracks in the church by creating a purely spiritual unity. It is doubtful whether there is anything in human life that can be called 'purely spiritual', without any need to express itself in material or physical form. Certainly in the Bible it is assumed that physical and spiritual life belong together in one whole. The unity of the church has to be both spiritual and material (that is, structural) at the same time. If the spiritual aspect alone is aimed at, and even if it is apparently achieved, disillusionment quickly sets in when one partner acts differently from the others in visible ways, as when a Protestant and a Roman Catholic are spiritually united (they think), and it is then discovered that the rules of one church forbid a member of the other to take communion at its altar. On the other hand, a purely structural union would be, of course, a miasmic illusion.

Unity then is both organic and organizational. It is also unity *in diversity*. If all Christians, or any other human beings, for that matter, came to believe exactly the same things, think in the same way and behave in identical fashion, it could be so only under the pressure of an outside force or personality (as seems to have been the case in Nazi Germany, and as can, alas, happen in other countries, too). In the united church of the future there will be great diversity of belief and practice, but we shall no longer unchurch those who think differently from ourselves within the orbit of Christian faith. It is time for the notion, 'unity = uniformity', to be finally quashed.

The recent succession of ecumenical disappointments in Britain has brought us back somewhere near to the beginning of the Ecumenical Movement in this country which had made such large advances. Another generation of Christians must go again through the process of mutual understanding and common worship which their predecessors experienced with joy and hope in their hearts. It is blasphemous to suggest that the recent setbacks were the will of God, but there has been some substantial gain in the midst of disappointment, since God brings good out of evil. Local Ecumenical Projects in England and Scotland keep alive the reality of unity in their own area, and by fellowship with each other across the regions of the country. Discussions of Roman Catholics with Anglicans, Methodists and 'Reformed' Christians are setting down the markers for future advance, and the World Council of Churches has put new life into the slow global movement towards unity by its publication of *Baptism, Eucharist and Ministry*. And the British Council of Churches is charting future progress from our present sad condition under the heading 'Not strangers but pilgrims'.

The 'holiness' of the church does not consist in the holy lives of its individual members, though it is exemplified and enhanced by them. Primarily, the holiness of the church means that it is called and set apart by God for special tasks; and secondly that this holiness is manifested in the love which is to be found among its members and in their approach towards human society and those who make it up. It is a tragedy that many of those who make the greatest claims to holiness show themselves to be the least loving. That is the charge made against the Puritans, historically, though it is not wholly justified, and it can be fairly levelled against groups and individuals in every age of the church. It is this that has given 'holiness' such a bad reputation. Holiness and love, for the Christian, are virtually the same thing. You cannot be holy without being loving; you cannot be loving without being holy.

'Catholicity' has to do with the wholeness of Christian faith. Wholeness of doctrine has been claimed by all churches from time to time, and by parties within each church; and some churches and parties include the claim in the name which they use of themselves. But the long and patient listening to the affirmations of other churches, and to their explorations of what they affirm, which is characteristic of the ecumenical age, has come near to persuading all churches that while all may claim some measure of catholicity, not one has it in its fullness. The catholicity of the church, in the full and proper sense, belongs to the future and not to the present. Certainly it was not to be found in the past either, for there were schisms in the early days, and there have been an increasing number as time has gone on, with every group that separated from the church claiming that it did so because the church had ceased to be catholic, and every church that dismissed its dissidents asserting that it alone possessed full catholicity. In each case the parent church has been impoverished by the separation, and in each case those who separated have been deprived, or have deprived themselves, of some of the elements of catholicity. Only the slow process of bringing together 'the separated brethren' – and we are all separated brethren – will create the catholicity which we all like to claim long before we have it, or even just after we have lost a great deal of it.

'Apostolicity' also can lead to exclusiveness. '*My* church is descended from the apostles – yours is not.' All churches within the Holy Catholic Church are descended from the apostles, but in all cases the line of descent has been frayed at some point or other, or even temporarily destroyed. Apostolicity shows itself in three main ways: continuity with the apostles in faith, life and ministry. Only when that threefold continuity is established and maintained in its entirety can the church, or any part of it, truly assert its apostolicity. But who could claim it now for any church, their own or another? The churches which are most

apostolic in life may be much less so in ministry; those who
are most apostolic in ministry (if that can ever be proved)
may be least apostolic in life and doctrine – and so on. Once
again there is a long and arduous process ahead of us if we
are to reach the goal.

There is a further meaning of the word 'apostolic' which
the authors of the creeds may or may not have intended. If
they did not, we must read it into the Creed. The apostles
received their name from the mission on which they were
sent by Jesus; they were 'those who were sent out'. If the
church is to resemble the apostles in this most important
particular of all, it must be 'sent out'. The church without
mission is like Shakespeare without his plays and his
poetry; or a museum piece of purely historical interest. The
Fathers at the councils may have been under the illusion
that the world was becoming steadily Christian, and so
have forgotten this meaning of apostolic. But we have our
illusions too, and one of the longest to survive is the illusion
that the mission is to individuals only and that the whole
task of mission is discharged if we are sufficiently evangel-
istic. The continuing mission of the church is to the whole
life of humankind.

A phrase in the Apostles' Creed which has dropped out
of the Nicene Creed is 'the communion of Saints'. It is
surprising that this is so; but the bishops in Constantinople
must have been preoccupied with other things. We can
restore the phrase in our minds as we say the Nicene Creed.
It points to the truth, not fully expressed in the clauses
about the church which the Nicene Creed does contain,
that the oneness of the church is not limited to this present
life, and that we are one family on earth and in heaven. This
is the basic truth; speculation will no doubt continue as to
the existence of purgatory as a stage on the way to heaven,
and as to the possibility of offering our prayers to the saints

in heaven who will then offer our prayers to God on our behalf. But we do not need to clear up these points before asserting the communion of saints.

'*We acknowledge one baptism for the forgiveness of sins.*' The ceremony of baptism is almost universally practised throughout the Christian church. Indeed, probably the only Christian communities who do not practise it are the Society of Friends and the Salvation Army, although other Christian denominations have sometimes made light of it. Since the evidence is strong that it was prescribed by Jesus, and was certainly practised from the very beginnings of the Christian mission, it is hard not to regard it as one of the constituent elements of the Christian church. And this, with due respect to the Quakers and the Salvation Army, is what the Creed does.

Mostly, it was the frequent abuse of the practice (and it has certainly been much abused) that turned the Quakers and the Salvationists against it, though the Quakers find theological difficulty in agreeing that particular sacraments are needful at all. No one should now have any difficulty in saying that both Quakers and Salvationists 'intend' for their members those things which other Christians seek in baptism, but express that intention without the rite. This leaves the theological status of both sets of Christians in relation to the mainstream churches in doubt, but this situation does not distress them; and scarcely anyone, surely, now believes that the unbaptized go in danger of damnation.

The almost universal practice of baptism with water in the name of the Trinity includes a great variety of interpretation; and the division of opinion and practice between those who baptize infants and those who baptize only those who have professed personal faith in Christ goes back at least to the time of the Reformation, and continues to this day.

The Creed asserts 'one baptism', clearly with the effect of saying that all baptism when properly practised is the same baptism – it is the baptism prescribed by Jesus as the sign of entry into the church (whether Jesus prescribed it in exactly these terms is, of course, doubtful, but it was not doubtful in the minds of the bishops in 381). The baptisms carried out by 'heretics' were questioned by many of those who remained orthodox (they were not 'properly' carried out, since the heretics did not really believe in the Trinity); the baptisms practised by the 'great church' were often questioned by those who separated from it, and vice versa. But we can now point to a near-consensus, at least in this country, that a baptism carried out in any church with water in the name of the Trinity is to be accepted by all churches; and the 'Common Certificate of Baptism' which can now be issued for every baptized person should eliminate any tendency on the part of any church to 'baptize' again someone baptized elsewhere, even in the form of 'If you have not been baptized, I baptize you in the name of the Father, the Son and the Holy Spirit.'

But the right age or stage of life for baptism is not settled to everyone's satisfaction yet. There is a disagreement, which may never be ended, about New Testament practice. Some say that only believers were baptized, others that the children of believing parents were baptized as well as believers. This difference of opinion roughly corresponds to the difference between those who think it quite wrong, since baptism in the New Testament, they claim, requires the response of faith to the grace of God before it is carried out, to baptize those who cannot yet have any faith; and those who believe that since the grace of God precedes any faith that we may have, and is the principal element in baptism, it is right and proper to bring people into the community of faith as soon as possible, so that they may grow up to have personal faith themselves in response to the continuing grace of God.

We may well not be able to agree about the New Testament evidence. But a reconciliation of conflict between paedobaptists and Baptists, so far as practice is concerned, may now be in sight. If we think of baptism as a one-off event which, when carried out, becomes just a fact in the past history of the person baptized, no reconciliation is possible. But if we come to see baptism as a *stage in the process of growth* in commitment to Christ in his church, then real progress can be made. For then we can suppose that the rite of baptism, signalizing above all things the grace of God, can come either at the beginning of this growth, giving the child his or her place in the family of the church where the growth, please God, takes place; or at the point in that growth, after Christian nurture in church and family, when he or she openly confesses his or her faith in Jesus Christ and the desire to take a full part in the life of the church.

It should go without saying that baptism, at whatever stage in Christian growth it takes place, cannot be repeated in any circumstances, and that no one should attempt to repeat it. For this would be to deny that the grace of God operated at and after the baptism, and this is a kind of affront to God. Yet in these days of 'charismatic renewal' it is natural that some people who have experienced the love and power of God in a new and special way should tend to suppose that their original baptism was worthless and that *now* is the time for real baptism. This is to misunderstand baptism as an occasion to mark a personal experience, rather than as an act of God's grace. Yet it is good that for those with this new experience there should be a service of self-dedication which cannot be confused with baptism. Confirmation may satisfy this need, or the Methodist

'Covenant Service', which has now spread from the church of its origin into many other churches. Some churches are in the process of creating a new service with all these considerations in mind.

'For the forgiveness of sins'. Many Christians are still content with the exact belief which this clause has certainly expressed for most Christians ever since the time of its promulgation – that each of us comes into the world in a state of 'original sin' which we inherit from our parents and forefathers, and ultimately from the first parents of the human race; and that baptism cleanses us from the guilt of that sin. But it is probable that a larger number of Christians now find it impossible to believe that at our very birth we are personally guilty before God and in need of forgiveness, and do not hold that the purpose of baptism can be truly conceived in these terms.

But it remains true that we inherit a nature which mostly finds wrongdoing easier than right-doing, and that it is not stretching things too far to say that our nature is 'sinful' (as well as being many other things, many of them good). Nor is it doubtful that at birth we enter into a world of human beings which is in many ways corrupt, so that we are shortly involved in choices when all the pressure is upon us to take a selfish course of action if we are to survive at all. This is described as 'the sin [not the sins] of the world' in John 1.29.

If this gives us a lead into a persuasive doctrine of original sin, what is the purpose of baptism in this regard? Can we claim to be cleansed by it from original sin? No, for there is at birth no guilt from which we need to be cleansed; but we *can* claim to have passed in baptism from the community of evil, which in the Gospel of John is called 'the world', into the community of good, which is the church, where the grace of God and the forgiveness of God through Christ are for ever made available to us, and the battle against our own self-centredness can best be fought.

So 'for the forgiveness of sins' means that the event of baptism points towards, and, by the imagery of water, clearly signifies, our cleansing from sin and the gift of new life – our 'forgiveness', in fact, which needs to be re-appropriated in repentance and faith every time we sin.

'Sin' is not an outdated concept, though many people prefer other names for it. It is not simply another word for 'wrongdoing'. 'Sin' is a religious word, not just a moral one; it has a reference to God every time it is used, for when we sin we are always, to a greater or lesser degree, rebelling against God. Sin is, in fact, an assertion of ourselves against God's rule over us. The Creed makes no distinction between our 'sin' and our 'sins', but it is useful to distinguish them in this way in our own minds: 'sin' is that within us which predisposes us to rebellion against God; 'sins' are our actual rebellious thoughts, or desires, or actions. The mercy and forgiveness of God, pre-figured in baptism, are offered to us for both.

'*We look for the resurrection of the dead*'. It is widely thought, by Christians and non-Christians alike, that Christianity teaches 'the immortality of the soul'. This is a highly reputable and venerable doctrine dating back in its de-veloped form to Plato, who lived over the turn of the fifth and fourth centuries BC. He held that there is a limited number of souls in the universe, each a pure and simple form of personal being; these souls have always been in existence and will never cease to exist; each of them inhabits a human body for a time, and leaves it at death; then, perhaps after a period of waiting, it passes into another human body, and so on for ever and ever.

But the Bible knows nothing of the separation of body and soul which this view requires (the passage read at

Remembrance Day services, 'the souls of the righteous are in the hand of God', lends colour to the idea, but it comes from the Book of Wisdom, a non-biblical writing greatly influenced by Platonism). For the Bible in both its parts the human person is one whole, with different capacities, some of which we should call spiritual, some mental, some physical. There is no question of the soul's living on after the body dies, for there is no separate entity, called a soul, which *can* live on.

This biblical view is obscured by a linguistic point. The chief biblical word for the total self is 'body', but it does not mean, clearly, what it means in ordinary English. 'Body' equals 'self', and when Paul speaks of the resurrection of the *body* he means the resurrection of the *self*.

Resurrection, be it noted, not immortality. There is no part of us, and nothing within us, which is naturally immortal. If we are to enter on the life to come, we need at death (or, as some think, on the Day of Judgment) to be raised up by God. And that is exactly what Jesus in the Gospel of John (6.39) and Paul in the fifteenth chapter of I Corinthians promises to us if we are 'in Christ'. It is possible, no doubt, by the use of a great deal of subtlety, and by cutting out the notion of 'the transmigration of souls' from Platonism, to reconcile Plato and Paul. But we are not at liberty to do this at the cost of suggesting that we have a *right* to eternal life. It is certainly the Christian position that such life is the gift of God, not our right or our achievement.

Many questions, of course, remain. Is there a resurrection for those who reject the Gospel, and what, if so, follows from their resurrection? Hell? The idea of a place or state of everlasting torment is nowadays so revolting to the Christian mind (it has not always been so) that those who go on believing in it prefer not to discuss it, or ease their susceptibilities by saying that no one, or almost no one, goes to hell. It is strongly urged by some modern Christians that we cannot entertain the idea that God's love is ever defeated, and that therefore in the end everyone finds the way to heaven. But some people have no wish for heaven, and are willing to forfeit it for the sake of earthly gain or pleasure or power; and others have, as far as we can see, deliberately shut themselves off from God. Are we to suppose that God forces heaven on them against their will? And if there are people who wilfully reject the love of God to the end, this is no defeat for love; for the essence of love is that it allows itself to be rejected, and still continues to be love.

If resurrection is the *gift* of God, it may be that we are entitled to conjecture (it cannot be more than conjecture, for the Bible gives no clear lead) that those who reject the gift of God, either blatantly or implicitly, simply – die?

But if we are 'raised', shall we be raised up at the moment of death, or at the Day of Judgment which follows the end of earthly history? This question has worried many people, perhaps appalled by the prospect of the long wait in nothingness which the second possibility seems to involve. But the question is not important after all, since, if we pass at death from time into eternity, there is no *time* between our death and the Last Judgment.

'*And the life of the world to come.*' Nearly all the theological and other books and treatises which purport to describe the life of heaven can be consigned to the waste paper basket. From the very nature of human life and thought, we cannot comprehend or imagine in advance the life to come. We can say a few important things on the basis of the love of God made known to us in Christ – that we shall be our true, matured selves, transformed, but still ourselves; that we shall be in community with each other; that we shall be consciously in the presence of God; that God will give us the appropriate means for the exercise of our powers. It is rash to say more.

But poetry can perhaps help us a little further on, for the poets have done better than the theologians in describing the indescribable. John Milton in *Lycidas*, on the death of a friend drowned at sea, says (we use his spelling and punctuation):

> . . . . Lycidas your sorrow is not dead,
> Sunk though he be beneath the watry floar.
> So sinks the day-star in the Ocean bed,
> And yet anon repairs his drooping head,
> And tricks his beams, and with new spangled Ore,
> Flames in the forehead of the morning sky:
> So Lycidas sunk low, but mounted high,
> Through the dear might of him that walk'd the waves,
> Where other groves and other streams along,
> With Nectar pure his oozy lock's he laves,
> And hears the unexpressive nuptiall song,
> In the blest Kingdoms meek of joy and love.
> There entertain him all the Saints above,
> In solemn troops, and Sweet Societies
> That Sing, and singing in their glory move
> And wipe the tears for ever from his eyes.

'Here and now, dear friends, we are God's children; what we shall be has not yet been disclosed, but we know that when it is disclosed we shall be like him, because we shall see him as he is' (I John 3.2).

Epilogue

The last creed of the church acceptable to all was adopted at Chalcedon, nearly fifteen hundred and fifty years ago. It is more than sixteen hundred years since the Nicene Creed was published in Constantinople. The Apostles' Creed is much older still.

They have certainly had a long run. It has to be remembered that for about a thousand years of their history they were imposed on all Christians everywhere on pain of excommunication or even death. Still, they have survived the split between East and West, the Reformation, the Anglican-Methodist separation, and many other divisions within the church. But has the long run now come to an end?

We have seen (or haven't we?) that the Nicene Creed, which is the centrepiece of credal confessions, needs some reinterpretation for our times; that reformulation at certain points would not come amiss; that there are serious omissions which need to be repaired; and that there are 'new' truths which are not recognized.

The great communions of Christendom see no need for scrapping the creeds. These vast spiritual corporations are often guilty of sheer conservatism, concealed under high-sounding names. But in this case they are doubtless right. The creeds still witness to basic principles of the faith, albeit, to us, sometimes obscurely.

Yet, however highly we may regard them, they cannot in

the end do more than mark a stage – a long and important one – in the exploration of Christian faith, and in apprehension of the truth as truth is in Jesus; they do not give the final solutions of every problem. Nowadays, moreover, the church faces not so much splits within itself (though the danger of those is not removed) as the splitting away of human society from the church.

This is a situation in which to go forward, not backward. The creeds provide the ground from which the church can go forward to a new statement of the faith, to the 'Common Expression of the Apostolic Faith Today', for which the World Council of Churches through its Faith and Order Commission is preparing us. And even, in due course and God's good time, to the first Ecumenical Council of the united church.

Appendix

The Apostles' Creed

I believe in God,
  the Father almighty,
  creator of heaven and earth.
I believe in Jesus Christ,
  his only Son, our Lord.
  He was conceived by the power of the Holy Spirit and
    born of the Virgin Mary.
  He suffered under Pontius Pilate, was crucified, died
    and was buried.
  He descended to the dead.
  On the third day he rose again.
  He ascended into heaven, and is seated at the right hand
    of the Father.
  He will come again to judge the living and the dead.
I believe in the Holy Spirit,
  the holy catholic Church,
  the communion of saints,
  the forgiveness of sins,
  the resurrection of the body,
  and the life everlasting. Amen.

The text of this is the one approved by the International
Consultation on English Texts, and now used in the
majority of English-speaking churches.

The Nicene Creed

We believe in one God,
    the Father, the almighty,
    maker of heaven and earth,
    of all that is, seen and unseen.
We believe in one Lord, Jesus Christ,
    the only Son of God,
    eternally begotten of the Father,
    God from God, Light from Light,
    true God from true God,
    begotten, not made,
    of one Being with the Father.
    Through him all things were made.
For us men and for our salvation
    he came down from heaven:
by the power of the Holy Spirit
    he became incarnate from the Virgin Mary,
    and was made man.
For our sake he was crucified under Pontius Pilate;
    he suffered death and was buried.
    On the third day he rose again
        in accordance with the scriptures;
    he ascended into heaven
        and is seated at the right hand of the Father.
He will come again in glory to judge the living and the
    dead, and his kingdom will have no end.
We believe in the Holy Spirit,
    the Lord, the giver of life,
        who proceeds from the Father and the Son.
    With the Father and the Son he is worshipped and
    glorified.
    He has spoken through the Prophets.
We believe in one holy catholic and apostolic Church.

We acknowledge one baptism for the forgiveness of sins.
We look for the resurrection of the dead,
    and the life of the world to come. Amen.

The text of this is the one approved by the International Consultation on English Texts, and now used in the majority of English-speaking churches, except that Orthodox churches leave out the phrase 'and the Son' in line 28.

The Chalcedonian Definition

Therefore, following the holy Fathers, we all with one accord teach men to acknowledge one and the same Son, our Lord Jesus Christ, at once complete in Godhead and complete in manhood, truly God and truly man, consisting also of a reasonable soul and body; of one substance with the Father as regards his Godhead, and at the same time of one substance with us as regards his manhood; like us in all respects, apart from sin; as regards his Godhead, begotten of the Father before the ages, but yet as regards his manhood begotten, for us men and for our salvation, of Mary the Virgin, the God-bearer; one and the same Christ, Son, Lord, Only-begotten, recognized in TWO NATURES, WITHOUT CONFUSION, WITHOUT CHANGE, WITHOUT DIVISION, WITHOUT SEPARATION; the distinction of natures being in no way annulled by the union, but rather the characteristics of each nature being preserved and coming together to form one person and subsistence, not as parted or separated into two persons, but one and the same Son and Only-begotten God the Word, Lord Jesus Christ; even as the prophets from earliest times spoke of him, and our Lord Jesus Christ himself taught us, and the creed of the Fathers has handed down to us.

Books for Further Reading

Those who would like to go more deeply into the historical and theological background and significance of the creeds should consult one or more of the following:

John Burnaby, *The Belief of Christendom*, SPCK 1959
J. N. D. Kelly, *Early Christian Creeds*, Longman 1972
Wolfgang Pannenberg, *The Apostles' Creed*, SCM Press 1972
Alan Richardson, *Creeds in the Making*, SCM Press 1935
Angela Tilby, *Won't You Join the Dance?*, SPCK 1985
Frances Young, *From Nicaea to Chalcedon*, SCM Press 1983

101

USes for a traditional Welsh hat

First Published 2022
© text and illustrations Huw Aaron, 2022

ISBN 978-1-91430-321-0

Published by Llyfrau Broga Books, Whitchurch, Cardiff